Twisted Logic

The Window of Depression

"Chaplain McDonald has done it again! By the Holy Spirit, she has captured the essence of the stronghold of depression. In this book, she not only reveals the spirit of depression, but also shines the light of the Lord on it. In this most engaging book, she put in place very practical prayers that anyone can pray and receive deliverance. The testimonies are as honest and insightful as the testimonies of the saints in the Bible that also suffered from depression. Just as God delivered them in the days of old, He, through His servant Chaplain McDonald, is delivering many from depression in this present day."

—Diedra Duncan, The Potter's House of Denver,
Road to Freedom, Table Leader

Vescinda McDonald

TWISTED LOGIC, THE WINDOW OF DEPRESSION

The books, audio books, eBooks, DVDs written and produced by Yong Hui V. McDonald are also available. Visit www.atlasbooks.com/griefpathway, (1-800-266-5564) or www.griefpwv.com or griefpwv@gmail.com or write to: GriefPathway Ventures LLC, P.O. Box 220, Brighton, CO 80601. Adora Productions is an imprint of the GriefPathway Ventures LLC.

Published by Adora Productions
Printed in the United States of America
ISBN: 978-1-935791-25-6
Cover Art & Design by Jorge Enciso, sodspro.com

First Printing: February 2011
1. Depression 2. Spiritual Healing
3. Spiritual Growth 4. Prayer
5. Christianity

ABOUT THE AUTHOR

Yong Hui V. McDonald, also known as Vescinda McDonald, a United Methodist minister, received her Master of Divinity from The Iliff School of Theology, and has been working as a chaplain at Adams County Detention Facility (ACDF) in Brighton, Colorado, since 2003. She is a certified American Correctional Chaplain, spiritual director, author, on-call hospital chaplain, and founder of the Transformation Project Prison Ministry (TPPM) in 2005. TPPM is a 501(c)(3) nonprofit and produces *Maximum Saints* books and DVDs containing transformation stories of inmates at ACDF. TPPM produced books and DVDs are distributed free of charge in jails, prisons and homeless shelters nationwide. Within six years, TPPM published eight English books, two Spanish translated books and produced four DVDs, and distributed more than 100,000 free copies of books and DVDs to prisons and homeless shelters nationwide. She founded GriefPathway Ventures LLC in 2010 to help others learn how to process grief and healing.

Education:

- Multnomah Bible College, B.A.B.E. (1984)
- Iliff School of Theology, Master of Divinity (2002)
- The Samaritan Counseling & Educational Center, Clinical Pastoral Education (CPE) (2002)
- Rocky Mountain Pastoral Care and Training Center (CPE) (2003)
- Formation Program for Spiritual Directors – (2004)

Books Written by Yong Hui V. McDonald:

- *Moment by Moment*
- *Journey With Jesus, Visions, Dreams, Meditations & Reflections*
- *Hope from Despair, Mystical Spiritual Experiences*
- *Dancing in the Sky, A Story of Hope for Grieving Hearts*
- *Twisted Logic, The Shadow of Suicide*
- *Dreams & Interpretations, Healing from Nightmares*
- *Twisted Logic, The Window of Depression*
- Compiled and published five *Maximum Saints* books under the Transformation Project Prison Ministry.

Producer: Produced the following DVDs:

- Two Maximum Saints DVDs
- *Dancing in the Sky, Mismatched Shoes*
- *Tears of Dragonfly, Suicide and Suicide Prevention*

CONTENTS

DEDICATION
ACKNOWLEDGMENTS

TWISTED LOGIC, THE WINDOW OF DEPRESSION

Chapter 1: Twisted Logic & Depression..........8

1. How did this book come about?
2. What is Twisted Logic?
3. What is Spiritual Oppression?
4. Depression and Twisted Logic
5. Medication and Depression
6. What does this book offer?
7. What motivated me to start writing this book?
8. What's the sign of recovery from depression?

Chapter 2: The Reasons for Depression..........15
The Pain that could cause Depression
1. Physical Pain
2. Emotional Pain
3. Spiritual Pain
(1) Twisted Logic
(2) Spiritual Oppression
1) Voices and Tormenting Spirits
2) Confusing Spirits
3) Accusing Spirits
4) Spirit of Despair & Suicide
5) Anger and Unforgiving Spirits
6) Spirit of Fear and Worry
7) Spirit of Obsession

Chapter 3: A Story of Recovery..........30
1. Despair
2. The Torment
3. Spiritual Power
4. An Accusing Spirit
5. A Turning Point
6. The Recovery
7. Delayed Healing
8. The Voice
9. Repentance
10. Blessings

Chapter 4: A Pinch of Faith..........44
1. "A PINCH OF FAITH" by Kelly Miller
2. "A WAKE UP CALL" by Raelyissa Angelino-Garnica
3. "ALL YOU NEED IS FAITH" by Cassidy Watkins

Chapter 5: Spiritual Counseling for the Depressed Minds 53
1. Guilt
2. The Pain
3. Sadness
4. Despair
5. Grief and Anger
6. Spiritual Deliverance
7. Grief and Hope
8. Spiritual Confusion
9. The Tormenting Spirit
10. Fear
11. The Voice
12. Bitterness

Chapter 6: Distressed People's Stories in the Bible.......75
1. Elijah

2. The King Saul
3. Jonah
4. Habakkuk
5. Nebuchadnezzar
6. Jesus
7. Paul

Chapter 7: Spiritual Prescription for the Depressed Minds..........85
1. Process Your Pains One by One
    (1) Anger & Unforgiving Heart
    (2) Grief & Loss
    (3) Abused & Traumatized
    (4) Self-Hate or Self-Mutilation
    (5) Despair & Suicidal Thoughts
    (6) Addiction, guilt or shame
    (7) Worry & Fear
2. Love God
3. Love Yourself
4. Meditate on the Word of God
5. Forgive Everyone
6. Resist Twisted Logic
7. Listen to the Voice of God
8. Develop a Relationship with the Holy Spirit
9. Serve Others
10. Proclaim Victory
    A Victory Prayer

Chapter 8: What Helps for Recovery...........129

Chapter 9: An Invitation..........130
1. An Invitation to Accept Christ
2. An Invitation to Transformation Project Prison Ministry (TPPM) & "One Million Dream Project"

DEDICATION

I dedicate this book to my Heavenly Father, my Lord and Savior Jesus Christ, and to the Holy Spirit. Also to all those who are in need of healing from hurts and pain.

ACKNOWLEDGMENTS

I thank God for my wonderful mother for her love and prayers for me. She prays for me and my ministry day and night. I believe that because of her prayers God has blessed me and my ministry beyond my imagination. She has been my cheerleader, and I thank God for a wonderful mother who has such love for all her children. She planted the seeds of faith and strength in my heart from my early childhood.

I am also deeply indebted to my wonderful husband Keith, who died in a car accident and is with the Lord. Keith brought healing in my heart and helped my ministry preparation more than anyone I've ever met. I thank God for giving me such a wonderful friend and husband for 30 years. I also thank my beautiful children. I pray that God will bless them beyond their imagination in all areas of life.

I am so grateful to all ACDF saints who helped me edit this book: Mary Diubaldo, Jeremy Dunn, Cara Frazic, Sara Gamez, Melinda Hudson, Raelyissa Angelino-Garnica, Heather Lopez, Melissa Saengaree, Veronica Sandoval, Jennifer Miklich, Arica Nichols, Jimmy Roberts- Perez, Jody Subia, Lakiesha Vigil, Charlayne Villagomez, Mireya Vizcarra, Mary Voogt, Cassidy Watkins and Georgette Wires. You all inspired me greatly and encouraged me in my writing project. Also, I thank Helen Sirios, Jody Nighswonger and sister Maureen Kehoe who helped me edit this book. Thank you and God bless you all!

Finally, I give glory and thanks to Jesus for giving me the privilege to write this book.

Chapter 1

Twisted Logic & Depression

1. *How did this book come about?*

My previous book, *Twisted Logic, The Shadow of Suicide* was written to help people who are affected by suicide or suicidal thoughts. It deals with many illogical destructive thoughts and voices people hear which I call twisted logic, and how they can experience healing by replacing these voices with life giving thoughts through God's Word. It was also written for people who are affected by suicide, to help them process grief and begin healing.

After the book was released, I saw the need for another book to help people who are depressed but not necessarily suicidal. There is a common theme among people who are depressed. Depressed people suffer from hopeless and helpless feelings. They lack motivation to go on and are immobilized with pain. Many depressed people not only suffer from emotional and mental pain but also spiritual pain. When people don't know how to process emotional and spiritual pain, they suffer greatly and they are in desperate need of help.

Since I started working as a chaplain at Adams County Detention Facility (ACDF) in 2003, I have learned that a jail is a lot like a spiritual hospital. Many people are stressed out, immobilized with pain, and are in need of spiritual healing and direction. I have counseled many people and have learned that many who are depressed are often suffering from destructive voices and spiritual oppression.

2. *What is Twisted Logic*?

Twisted Logic is any destructive, hurtful, illogical, confusing and negative thoughts or voices that come to our minds. They are contrary to God's values and the Word of God. The Word of God brings us conviction, forgiveness, hope, peace, spiritual freedom, healing and transformation. Twisted logic can promote worries, fear, turmoil, confusion misery, hopelessness, helplessness, despair and deep emotional pain which can lead to spiritual pain and depression.

In this book, I will refer to twisted logic as destructive thoughts, destructive voices, wrong thoughts, confusing thoughts, confusing voices, hurtful thoughts, hurtful voices, twisted thoughts, twisted thinking, and twisted voices.

3. *What is Spiritual Oppression*?

Spiritual oppression has supernatural influences and the origin is the devil and demons. People can feel physically attacked and even tormented to the point that they feel so much pain without any physical reason. They hear voices in their mind and sometimes they are audible. Some people feel that something is attacking them even though they may not see it. Some may see who is attacking them. People can be spiritually attacked while sleeping and they might think they are just having nightmares.

Many people do not realize that these spiritual attacks cause them to become confused and scared. They don't know how to free themselves from these attacks. They think it's a natural phenomenon. Consequently, they don't seek God for healing. The Word of God has all the answers and directions for healing from spiritual oppression.

4. *Depression and Twisted Logic*

From both my personal and ministry experiences, confused thoughts combined with spiritual oppression can cause severe depression. Severe depression can lead a person to suicidal thoughts which I call the "red zone" in my book, *Twisted Logic, The Shadow of Suicide*.

People who are in the red danger zone are in so much pain that they think ending their lives will end the pain. That concept itself is twisted thinking. God can bring healing and free people from emotional and spiritual pain. People who are not suicidal but depressed, are in the yellow danger zone and need healing. If left untreated, they could move into the red zone.

5. *Medication and Depression*

I believe God has given different gifts to different people to help people experience healing. Medical doctors are working very hard to bring healing to people who are depressed. We should not undermine what they do. I want to make sure that you understand that this book doesn't replace your medication. This book is focused on emotional and spiritual healing. Not all depression is caused by destructive thoughts or twisted thinking. Some people may have a neurological illness or a chemical imbalance that they have no control over. Medication can help both their thoughts and behaviors.

6. *What does this book offer?*

Among the depressed people I have met, many have suffered from the side effects of medication. Some side effects such as feeling numb or feeling happy all the time to the point of exhaustion may lead some patients to discontinue their medication. Also, some quit their anti-depressant medicine because of suicidal thoughts or violent reactions.

What can a depressed person do to help themselves when taking medication is not an option? What about those who suffer from destructive voices and cannot benefit from anti-depressant medicine? What about people who are spiritually oppressed and are in need of spiritual freedom? Is there any spiritual guidance on how to overcome destructive voices and spiritual oppression? This book is an attempt to answer these questions. It will give you some understanding, insight and spiritual guidance on how to process your emotional and spiritual pain that is caused by destructive voices and spiritual oppression.

7. *What motivated me to start writing this book?*

Recently, one of my friends whom I will call Julia, (not her real name), who used to be very effective in ministry was struggling with depression. Her anti-depression medication was causing her confusion. She shared that after taking the medication she found herself outside in the middle of the night. She didn't even remember how she got there. She was scared and stopped taking the medication. Julia felt lost and thought about admitting herself to a mental hospital. That's when she called me. God gave me the Scripture to read for her just before she came to my home. It was Joshua chapter 1:3–9. I understood why she needed that Scripture after I heard what was happening to her. This is how she described her pain when she arrived at my home:

> "There's a crying out so deep within me that my spirit, mind, and body no longer function. I can't think straight. My emotions are very high and low. My body is very, very tired and weak. My heart is filled with pain, hurt and sorrow. My eyes are

blurred. My heart is blocked. My thoughts of fear make me paralyzed at times. Empty, dry, broken and anguished, I cry out to God. Help me!" - Julia

When Julia arrived, she was confused and suffering from a foggy mind. That is one of the signs of spiritual confusion caused by destructive voices and spiritual oppression. While she spent three days in my home, I helped her to process her painful issues one by one through reflection, meditation on the Scriptures, prayer, repenting, forgiveness, recognizing destructive thoughts and resisting them. Also, she rebuked the confusing spirits to leave her in the name of Jesus and asked God for freedom from spiritual oppression.

My son, a student of University of Colorado, saw how Julia looked down and gloomy when she arrived at my home. The second day she stayed in my home he whispered to me, "Mom, tell her to take anti-depression medicine."

I replied, "That's a good suggestion, but her problem is not a chemical imbalance. She already tried medicine and it didn't work. Her problem is a spiritual problem. Spiritual problems cannot be solved with medication."

The second day, God asked Julia to write a confession letter. As far as she can remember that was the first time she had heard God's voice. She started writing. It helped her to cleanse her soul and continue her healing process.

The next day her foggy mind started to clear. After she processed many areas that had piled up in her mind, she had a breakthrough and found peace, joy, meaning and purpose for which she never had when she suffered from depression.

Before Julia left, I had given her spiritual

prescriptions which I added in chapter seven of "Spiritual Prescription for the Depressed Minds." The prescriptions I used to help Julia is what I use when I counsel depressed people at ACDF and as a hospital chaplain. I have seen many who recovered from depression when they followed the spiritual prescription.

The third day, my son had noticed that Julia had gone through a transformation. After Julia left, my son said, "That was a quick healing."

I replied, "I knew God could do it. She is learning how to resist destructive voices with the Word of God. She will be fine."

God has all the resources to help people who suffer from spiritual pain available through the Scriptures. However, I have learned that many people don't seem to realize it. I want to share what I have learned from my ministry to help others. That's what has motivated me to write this book.

8. *What's the sign of recovery from depression*?

Healing from hurtful thoughts and spiritual oppression is a process. People who recover from depression have a new perception of "hope" which they didn't have earlier. Also, applying the Word of God and processing pain give them clarity from a foggy mind. It helps people to gain emotional and spiritual strength. It also helps them to relieve emotional and spiritual pain and torment. They are able to function better, to smile, and to start seeing beauty in themselves, others and life. They can find joy in life which they didn't have before when they suffered from depression.

Conclusion

I believe our perception is like having a window in a room where we are trying to see the beauty through the glass. In order to see not only the beauty in ourselves but the beauty in others and the beauty of life, the glass window needs to be clear. This window is our hearts. Our hurts, pain, sufferings, and twisted thoughts can cloud the window.

Many people's windows have been clouded with so much pain and twisted thoughts that they cannot see things clearly nor see the beauty of people or the beauty of life. Here is good news: God can help us clear our hearts to see the beauty that we are meant to see.

Healing from a depressed mind is like seeing things through a clear window and seeing the beauty we weren't able to see earlier. This healing is possible through God and meditation on His Words. He has not only done it for me but for many others that I have come to know. He can also do it for you.

Chapter 2

The Reasons for Depression

Many people who are suffering from depression are in turmoil and suffer from pain. There are different reasons people suffer from pain. I will share three kinds of pain that can lead people to a depressed mind and into deep depression if they don't know how to process their pain.

Three Kinds of Pain

1. Physical Pain

(1) Physical illness: When people suffer from prolonged illness and pain and feel there is no hope to be cured, they might get depressed.

(2) Neurological or chemical problems: A person who suffers from neurological or a chemical imbalance can be led to depression.

2. Emotional Pain

(1) Death and loss of their loved ones: When people lose their loved ones, they can be emotionally paralyzed in pain. Depending on the relationship the person had with the deceased person, he/she may suffer from feelings of guilt, anger, resentment, loneliness, or many other emotions that they need to process. When people cannot process their grief and loss, they can become depressed. Healing from pain caused by loss is possible with God. When they start reading the Bible and start processing their grief and pain, they can experience healing.

(2) Death of a relationship: People who don't know how to

deal with grief and loss from a broken relationship often become depressed.

(3) Feelings of unworthiness: When a person suffers from helplessness, hopelessness, disappointment, boredom, guilt, shame, an unforgiving spirit, or self-hatred and despair for a long period, they can become depressed.

(4) Addiction problems: A person who suffers from substance abuse like alcohol and drugs, even some prescription drugs, can be led to open the door of depression and twisted thinking. People are vulnerable when they lose control of their mind and thoughts. That's what addiction does. Some people turn to alcohol and drugs when they are in emotional pain. This only delays the healing process. People are vulnerable to spiritual oppression when they are under the influence of drugs and alcohol.

(5) Financial problems: When people have financial problems, they can become distressed. They may feel that they have no way out and can become depressed.

(6) Other's rejection: People need love and acceptance. Sometimes those who do not receive it from their significant others, especially from their family and friends, can become depressed.

(7) Lack of purpose and direction in life: When people do not have clear goals on how to live a fulfilling life and suffer from boredom can become depressed. Some people try to fill their empty heart with things, people, jobs, or even alcohol and drugs.

(8) Prolonged extreme stress and abusive situations: When people suffer from intense pain and ongoing stress such as war, incarceration, a natural disaster, value conflict, mental illness and abusive situations, they are emotionally, mentally, and spiritually exhausted and can become depressed if they don't process their pain,

issues and situations.

(9) Inability to process anger and forgiveness: People who don't know how to forgive others or how to handle anger constructively can become depressed.

(10) People who lack self love and self forgiveness: When people have no love or respect for themselves and do not forgive themselves, they can become depressed.

3. Spiritual Pain

Depression can be caused by spiritual pain. People who are overwhelmed with problems in life and suffer from emotional pain are more vulnerable to spiritual pain. Spiritual pain is caused by twisted logic and also spiritual oppression.

Two Causes of Spiritual Pain:

(1) Twisted Logic

Destructive thoughts start in our minds. Our mind is a spiritual battlefield. That's where confused thoughts can be planted, watered, and put a person in a spiritual prison of pain and torment. The more you have accepted destructive thoughts, the more you are in emotional and spiritual turmoil and pain.

People hear voices that are contrary to the Word of God in their mind. One of the spirits working hard in people is a spirit of despair. When people face challenging situations, these people suffer from negative thoughts telling them that life is not worthwhile and there is no hope for them. God can help us overcome our challenging situations.

Many suffer from devaluing themselves and life in general, as well as other people's lives. These voices usually come as thoughts to our mind but can also be an audible voices. These voices don't give people comfort but depressed thoughts instead and lead people to despair. When people accept these voices they can be filled with despair, sadness, anger, hopelessness, helplessness and many other negative thoughts and feelings to the point of immobilization.

Paul talks about how our battle is in our mind. *"For though we live in the world, we do not wage war as the world does. The weapons we fight with are not the weapons of the world. On the contrary, they have divine power to demolish strongholds. We demolish arguments and every pretension that sets itself up against the knowledge of God, and we take captive every thought to make it obedient to Christ." (2 Corinthians 10:3-5)*

Through God's help and the prescription from the Word of God, we can experience healing from emotional and spiritual pain. We can resist these voices and see the brighter side of what God can offer.

The Source of Twisted Logic

We are affected by many different sources. There are six ways we can be affected. The following are how the spirit of despair can affect our mind.

1) We devalue ourselves.
2) Our family values and principles which do not value people or encourage us to value ourselves.
3) Many destructive thoughts have supernatural origin. The devil plants the seed of despair in people's heart to devalue life and themselves.
4) Culture and media can promote devaluing certain groups of people. It can promote people to devalue themselves and others.
5) Friends and other people who do not value us and that can negatively affect us.

6) Religious beliefs that do not value people and can be used to hurt other people.

Twisted thinking may have started through our sinful nature, spiritual ignorance or rebellious heart like what Adam and Eve did in the garden. There are many reasons for this:

1) Our illogical thinking
2) Lack of understanding of people or the situation
3) Not being able to see the big picture from a spiritual point of view
4) A selfish and rebellious heart from our sinful nature
5) Lack of knowledge of the Scripture
6) Lack of common sense

When we start twisting the Word of God, the devil can twist it more and even affect our spiritual walk with the Lord. That's why it is so important to know God's values and know what is good and bad according to the Bible and obey the Lord.

<u>Family influences</u>: Adam was with Eve so he went along with his wife and disobeyed the Lord instead of correcting her or trying to stop her. Anything that tries to justify our sins goes against the Word of God, brings pain and turmoil and is twisted thinking by nature. Adam and Eve failed the test of obedience. They started twisting the Word of God. They trusted their own judgment, and listened to the devil's destructive voice instead of obeying the Word of God.

<u>The devil</u>: Not all the negative voices we hear in our mind are from the devil. We can also devalue ourselves. But when you hear voices in your mind that you know it's not your thought but hear clearly that you are no good, it is likely you are hearing the voice of the devil. The Bible tells

us that the devil is an accuser. *"Then I heard a loud voice in heaven say: 'Now have come the salvation and the power and the kingdom of our God, and the authority of his Christ. For the accuser of our brothers, who accuses them before our God day and night, has been hurled down.'"* (Revelation 12:10)

Jesus was also tested by the devil who twisted the meaning of the Scriptures. The devil tried to encourage Jesus to commit suicide by falling from a high place, and used the Scripture that the angels would save him. Jesus said we are not supposed to test God. *(Luke 4:12)* We can learn from Jesus how to fight the twisted interpretation of God's powerful living Word. The devil also knows the Scriptures and twists them to make us fall into sin by appealing to our sinful nature.

People who are deceived by the devil's lies can hurt themselves and others. When they start applying the Scriptures to fight the devil's temptation like what the Lord did, they can win the spiritual battle and find peace.

The devil has not retired yet and our sinful nature can lead us to fall into sin if we are not equipped to fight using God's Word. The devil has been planting the seed of illogical thinking from the beginning, working to plant the seed of doubt and twisting the truth even now. He still tricks people to hurt and kill through the same lies. We need to be aware that we are in a constant spiritual battle moment by moment, but God provides all the resources and weapons to fight in the Word of God.

Our culture: Not all of our cultural values are bad. There are many good values. God has given each of us a conscience. A desire to be good and a desire to be good to others. However, if people who are affecting our values and moral standard do not have God's values, their values can be affected by twisted thinking.

Any kind of prejudice or disrespect against others,

whether it will be in color, gender, age or any form which devalues other human being is against God's values. God created everyone equal, precious, and according to God's image. Unfortunately, some people have different ways of looking down on others to elevate themselves. This is sin. We need to learn to value each other as God values everyone.

Media: We need to watch out for what we see and hear. Media is a good example of the kind of values people represent. It can help us learn and develop good morals if people who develop media have God's values and standards. However, there are many who do not have God's values and go against the Word of God. Sometimes their values are twisted values. Music, books, art and other resources can affect our values. Other's spirituality can affect our spiritual condition if we continuously have exposure to them.

Other people: What we hear from the people whom we value affects us negatively or positively. Unfortunately, if we don't have much knowledge of God's values, others who do not have God's values can influence us with wrong values and thinking that go against the Word of God. Paul warns us about this. He wrote, *"Do not be misled: 'Bad company corrupts good character.' Come back to your senses as you ought, and stop sinning; for there are some who are ignorant of God--I say this to your shame." (1 Corinthians 15:33-34)*

Religion: Some people may say that they believe in God, but they don't understand how twisted thoughts can affect their thinking and behaviors. A partial truth can hurt us when people start to twist the Word of God to fit their own sinful lifestyle. We need to be aware that other believer's values, even religious leaders, do not always reflect the Word of God and the truth. It can be affected by their sinful nature and lack of understanding of God's truth.

The spiritual leaders in Jesus' time believed that Jesus had to die. They came up with many accusations. Religious leaders were jealous and eventually handed Jesus over to be crucified. Condemning an innocent person with lies is sin. Justifying any sinful thought and behavior by using the Scripture or without Scripture is not what God wants us to do.

When people used the Scriptures to teach about God but neglected teaching the whole truth, Jesus rebuked them: *"Woe to you Pharisees, because you give God a tenth of your mint, rue and all other kinds of garden herbs, but you neglect justice and the love of God. You should have practiced the latter without leaving the former undone."* (Luke 11:42)

Paul said, *"See to it that no one takes you captive through hollow and deceptive philosophy, which depends on human tradition and the basic principles of this world rather than on Christ."* (Colossians 2:8)

Being healed from twisted logical thinking is a process of finding out where we have been deceived, and changing it into God's life-giving Words to heal the wounds. It will take time to process. You should not be discouraged when you are not released from pain immediately. Spiritual healing is a process of taking care of areas with God's help. It's hard work with reflection and meditation, but it's worth it. Living with twisted thinking brings only misery and pain.

(2) Spiritual Oppression

Many people who are depressed suffer from spiritual attacks. Understanding what we are struggling with can guide us on how to fight the voices we hear in our minds. There are many different voices of destructive thoughts that can immobilize us. The following are some examples of how some people can suffer from voices and spirits that attack them. When a person accepts them, they can be depressed. Also, spiritual oppression can lead people to a foggy mind which can affect their concentration. God can bring healing. The Word of God has the answer to fight those voices and attacks.

1) Voices and Tormenting Spirits

Tormenting spirits attack people in two different ways. The first one is through voices in our mind. It can give destructive suggestions so people are confused or in turmoil. When they accept the voices and follow them, they will fall into more turmoil. This can open the door to tormenting spirits where a person can suffer from deep emotional pain.

People who suffer from spiritual pain may or may not be overwhelmed with problems in life, but they suffer from spiritual pain caused by a spiritual attack.

The attack can happen day and night. Many people are attacked when they are asleep through nightmares. Again, you can depend on the Lord for healing through His Word, prayer and rebuking the demon.

People who suffer from tormenting spiritual attacks may have accepted these destructive voices. They need to process the issues that are overwhelming to them one by one with the Word of God to experience healing.

The second way tormenting spirits attack is with physical pain. People feel pain, but in reality they don't have any physical problems. Although, in some cases, they can have physical problems caused by demons. When the demons leave, these people are healed. Many people don't realize that their deep pain is caused by these tormenting spirits.

People who are attacked by tormenting demons

need to rebuke the demon in Jesus' name in faith. This will enable them to be released from the tormenting demon. If the demon doesn't leave right away, even after rebuked in Jesus' name, look into it to see if there is anything that you are missing.

Lack of faith in God or living in sin can cause the devil to still have a hold on you. Repent and take care of sin and have faith in God so you can be strong and free from the tormenting demons. There may be many issues that you need to process and let them go. Ask the Lord what you need to do to experience healing.

2) Confusing Spirits

Another way the devil torments is to confuse people through showing them the spiritual realm. The devil showed Jesus the whole world and tried to convince him to worship Satan. Some people can not only hear, but see and feel the spiritual world.

Some people who don't understand or believe that the spiritual world may exist think that they are losing their mind when they encounter spiritual beings. Some may feel the dark shadow hovering over them and cannot focus or concentrate.

When people are bombarded with so many thoughts, especially painful and negative thoughts, they can be affected by foggy minds which are caused by confusing spirits. People need to take the time to reflect and process their hurts and pain to find healing through the Word of God. Through prayer, they can be free from confusing spirits.

As they process issues, they need to let go and solve these issues according to the Word of God. Rebuking the spirit of confusion in the name of Jesus, they can find clarity and be freed from a foggy mind.

3) Accusing Spirits

People who are suffering from accusing spirits hear the voices in their mind saying that they are no good and cannot be forgiven. Therefore, they are anxious and feel hopeless, helpless and worthless. Again, these voices are against the Word of God.

There is a difference between conviction of sins by the Holy Spirit and accusing voices. When the Holy Spirit convicts us of our sins, we are remorseful and understand our sin. When we repent, God forgives us. We are free from guilt and shame.

Even after we ask God for forgiveness, the accusing spirit tells us that we are horrible people and that God cannot forgive us. Don't believe it. This is a lie from the devil.

Jesus died on the cross to forgive us. What He did on the cross wipes away our sins and cleanses us if we repent and ask for forgiveness. The accusing spirits can put people in prisons of guilt, shame and self-hatred. When they learn how to resist the accusing voice with God's Word, they can find freedom from painful thoughts.

Unfortunately, many believers suffer from accusing voices. The devil can twist the meaning of the Word of God to accuse people and make them feel worthless. We need to have faith in the Word of God not in accusing voices.

4) Spirit of Despair and Suicide

The spirit of despair tries to convince people to devalue themselves and others. What God created is good and people are God's masterpiece among creatures. Any thoughts that devalues yourself and others, you have to realize where they are coming from and resist them.

If you don't know how to resist the spirit of despair the next strong demon of suicide and murder can try to convince you to commit self-murder.

When people hear voices of suicidal thoughts and don't know how to resist them, they may follow the devil's suggestions and kill themselves even though they had no intention of killing themselves.

Jesus comes to free the spiritual prisoners from darkness. We, believers of God, have that power to resist anything that hinders loving God, loving ourselves and loving others. Our knowledge of the Scripture will give us discernment on what is right and wrong in God's eyes. Without fear of the Lord and knowledge of the Scripture, we fail to recognize the enemies destructive voices. That's how we can fall into sin.

5) Anger and Unforgiving Spirits

Many people do not realize the power of forgiveness. It frees us from tormenting demons and it will free us from focusing on human weaknesses and sin. We need to focus on Christ and His commands and obey Him by forgiving and blessing others.

Many people who are depressed suffer from anger, resentment, bitterness and have an unforgiving spirit. There are times that we are not willing to forgive and we justify our unforgiving heart. That's our sinful nature working in us.

This is one area that the devil will use to put people in bondage when they decide not to forgive. When we open the door to the devil, we lose peace. We can be immobilized with pain and agony. As long as we don't forgive, we are letting the devil influence our thoughts and behaviors. When we decide to forgive, the demons lose power over us.

Sometimes even though people want to forgive and they have made a decision to forgive, they just can't. They are constantly reminded of what happened to them and they struggle to let go of the past. When that happens, know that you are in a spiritual battle. Ask the Lord for forgiveness for holding resentment and give that person to the Lord. God understands your heart and He will forgive you. Rebuke the spirit of unforgiveness in Jesus' name. What's important is to try to obey the Lord. Understand that forgiveness is a process, so it might take time, but with God's help you can forgive and be freed from the spirit of unforgiveness.

6) Spirit of Fear and Worry

Many people are affected by the spirit of worry and fear. Many times these worries and fears may be valid, but in most cases they aren't.

Some people have been traumatized and need to process their hurts and need healing from memories and events that happened to them. Their worries and fears are based on their experiences. They need healing from the Lord.

Some, however, do not have reason to worry or fear and are not traumatized. They hear voices telling them that there are things to worry about.

People cannot have peace while living in fear. When we turn to God, He gives us peace. Many people do not realize that the spirit of worry and fear is planting the thoughts of worry and fear. People can be paranoid for no reason and try to isolate themselves from others. We need to examine what we hear. God can heal our mind and heart from worry and fear. Meditating on the Word of God will chase away the spirits of worry and fear.

7) Spirit of Obsession

People who suffer from obsession have a difficult time controlling their thoughts. They focus on something that they know is harmful to their emotional, mental and spiritual well being. Any kind of addiction has to be closely examined. The spirit of obsession may have been holding them so tight to the point that they feel they cannot overcome addictive thoughts and addictive behaviors.

They need to be delivered from the spirit of obsession and impure thoughts, repent their life-style and turn to the Lord for help. Then, they can gain control over their own thoughts and life. People who are traumatized or have addictions are very vulnerable to opening the doors to this spirit. With God's help they can be delivered from it.

Grief and loss can bring so much pain and immobilize people. When people lose their loved ones it's natural to grieve, but if mourning for the loss becomes their daily routine, they are suffering from the spirit of despair. When people lose their loved ones through death or divorce, they may think that there is no reason to live. There are many areas that grieving people need to process so they can eventually let go of the person to God's care.

Recognizing that what we receive is not ours but is a temporary gift from God makes us have a perspective that God wants us to have. God is the one who provides hope in every situation, even in the midst of pain and loss. Job's reaction to grief and loss can teach us how to handle our grief and loss. Also, Job's wife's anger teaches us that when we value people and things more than God, we can become angry at God in times of grief and loss.

Conclusion

God does not want us to be depressed and suffer from painful thoughts. He wants us to have peace and joy. Jesus wants us to have an abundant life to the fullest.

We believers of Jesus have received the power and authority over the demons. *"The seventy-two returned with joy and said, 'Lord, even the demons submit to us in your name.' He replied, 'I saw Satan fall like lightning from heaven. I have given you authority to trample on snakes and scorpions and to overcome all the power of the enemy; nothing will harm you."* (Luke 10:17-19) *"And these signs will accompany those who believe: In my name they will drive out demons; they will speak in new tongues."* (Mark 16:17)

We need to guard our hearts and recognize what kind of spirit is after us so we can fight it with the Word of God and resist the spirit in Jesus' name.

Reflection

1) Did you see areas where you are affected by confused thoughts or spirits that are oppressing you? Which ones seem to describe your condition?
2) What do you think you should do to experience healing? If you think you need a medical doctor, professional counselor, mental health, social worker, pastor or chaplain for counseling, don't wait. Contact them immediately.
3) Pray to ask the Lord for spiritual wisdom, knowledge, understanding, discernment and direction so you can experience healing from a depressed mind.

Prayer: "God of love and compassion, please help me sort out my problems according to your wisdom. Help me see myself as you see me so I can repent and clean my heart to experience healing. I pray that you will free me from all my worries and fears. Help me to experience your joy and peace in the name of Jesus Christ who died for me so I can be forgiven and have eternal life. Help me to process my pain one by one. Holy Spirit, guide me in my healing process so I can focus on loving the Lord. Amen."

Chapter 3

A Story of Recovery

1. Despair

I was deeply depressed in my early twenties after my sister died in a car accident. That was the most difficult time in my life. I was immobilized with pain and grief. I was already suffering from the spirit of despair before I lost my sister. My alcoholic father's violent temper and his abusive behaviors were the cause of my despair.

The loss of my sister triggered deep emotional wounds which I had been carrying for so long. My difficult childhood trauma of watching my father beat my mother opened the door for the spirit of resentment, anger, bitterness, helplessness and hopelessness.

I remember once he tried to burn my mother's skin with a cigarette and I stopped him. I was in shock. How could a person devalue another human being and hurt them, especially their family? I couldn't understand it. I hated my father and slowly started believing that life was not worthwhile. I thought everyone suffered and there was no hope in life.

At the time, I didn't realize my depression was related to what I had accepted in my mind – twisted thinking. The reason I suffered so much pain was because I didn't know how to fight these destructive voices. I had attended church all my life and believed in God, but I neglected reading the Bible.

I also suffered from the spirit of worry and fear for many years. I would constantly worry about what would happen at home every day and wondered if I could go to sleep peacefully at night.

2. The Torment

Not only did I suffer from voices of despair, worry and fear. I also suffered from emotional and spiritual pain caused by tormenting demons day and night. Whenever my sister appeared in my dreams, toward the end, something would always be choking me. I had a difficult time breathing. I was calling God to help me, but I couldn't wake up right away.

These nightmares terrified me. I couldn't sleep well so during the day I suffered from severe headaches. Then, my mother would put her hands on me and pray for me. My headaches would disappear.

My mother told me that it wasn't my sister appearing in my dream, but a demon was appearing like my sister and attacking me by choking me. I finally realized that there is a spiritual world. During those days I don't know how and why, but my spiritual eyes were opened. I saw demonic faces in other people's faces. I was so confused and suffered from a foggy mind. I had a difficult time concentrating on anything. My mother told me to read the Bible when I was suffering from depression. That was the best advice I ever received from anyone.

3. Spiritual Power

After I started reading the Bible, I realized that the Word of God had spiritual power. For the first time in my life I realized that I was a sinner. I always thought I was a good person. I never got in trouble at home or school.

This was a new experience for me. I asked God for forgiveness in tears and found peace which I never thought existed.

I had been a reader since I was little. I read so many

interesting philosophy and psychology books but didn't give me answers about life or the purpose of my life. They caused more confusion and despair.

The Word of God gave me hope and direction. I never experienced anything like that when I read other books. I started understanding that there is purpose and meaning in life. The more I read the Bible, the more I was able to have a new perspective of hope in life and gain spiritual strength. Somehow, my spiritual condition was affecting my physical health. As I gained more spiritual insight, I got stronger physically.

I was amazed at what God could do through the Word of God. I carried the Bible everywhere and read it. My mind became clearer as I read the Bible.

I wanted to study the Bible more and that's why I started attending Suwon Bible College. Even when I was attending school, I had not completely recovered from the spiritual attacks and many things I had suffered at home with my father didn't get resolved. I still had a difficult time focusing on the positive aspects of my life.

4. The Accusing Spirit

I experienced something new in my spiritual journey. I learned that not only can the Holy Spirit use the Bible to give me strength, but the devil can also use the Scripture to confuse me and bring turmoil in my heart. I started hearing voices of condemnation.

I had already confessed my sins and had been forgiven by God and experienced peace prior to that. The Holy Spirit's conviction of sins brought me forgiveness, peace and joy. The devil's accusing voice made me feel guilt and shame with no hope but despair and turmoil.

I was confused at first because I didn't know where these voices came from. The voices told me that I was no good and God could not forgive me. This was contrary to the Word of God. When I heard these voices, I was in turmoil and became discouraged, so I knew it was not from the Lord.

I realized that this is another one of the devil's tricks to make me focus on my past sins which God does not remember any more.

I began to recognize the accusing spirits who used the Scriptures to accuse me. I started fighting these voices with the Word of God. One of the Scriptures that encouraged me in this spiritual battle was Paul's letter to the Romans. In chapter seven. He describes how much he agonized with his sinfulness and felt helpless. Then he turned to God and claimed victory by pointing out what Jesus had done for him.

Paul wrote, *"Therefore, there is now no condemnation for those who are in Christ Jesus, because through Christ Jesus the law of the Spirit of life has set me free from the law of sin and death." (Romans 8:1-2)*

After I started resisting the accusing voices with the Word of God, I was eventually freed from the accusing spirits and found peace.

5. A Turning Point

Recovering from deep depression was a slow and long process. My nightmares disappeared but I was not completely freed from the tormenting spirits. I was still suffering the devil's attack and had a difficult time concentrating. My foggy mind needed healing.

The first year I was attending Suwon Bible College, I had spiritual encounters which I didn't expect. When I saw people I could tell if they were working with demons. I saw a demon's face in their faces. It scared me. These spirits wouldn't just let me walk by, but they attacked me. I felt it in my body. I was literally being beaten physically by the spirit which caused me fear and anguish. I was so exhausted that by the time I got home, I felt like collapsing on the floor.

My mother would pray for me and then I would gain strength and be able to get up. I experienced the power of prayer through my mother. I felt an evil presence when the devil was present and with those who were working with demons. This was something new to me. I was experiencing the spiritual world.

One night I visited a friend and the devil attacked me physically all night long. Whenever I tried to go to sleep, I couldn't sleep at all. The only thing I could do to protect myself from the attack was to pray and rebuke the demons. I still suffered from many destructive voices and I couldn't concentrate, so my grades in Bible college were poor.

My turning point came when I started reading Watchman Nee's *Spiritual Man* at one of my school friend's home. The light came on when I started reading this book. It describes how the devil and the Holy Spirit can speak to our minds, and shows us that our minds are a spiritual battlefield. I needed to recognize the origin of the voices and resist the devil's lies.

That was a revolutionary moment in my life. His spiritual insight gave me understanding of why I was suffering from spiritual attacks even though I was reading the Bible and praying. I had no idea that I had to guard my thoughts to be freed from destructive thoughts.

I didn't know much about spiritual battles at the time. Consequently, I accepted the devil's lies and didn't even realize it. Therefore, I believed the thoughts of despair were my thoughts. Instead of resisting them, I accepted them. Consequently, I opened the door to the tormenting demons.

The destructive voice I accepted in my mind was that life means only suffering and pain. Therefore, life was not worthwhile. There were no thoughts about how God has plans to bring hope and healing. There was no room for Jesus' intention of providing us with abundant life if I accept these voices of despair.

I finally realized that I accepted too many confusing thoughts from many books which didn't have spiritual insights. Also, Korean culture doesn't value women and that contributed to the twisted thinking that my life is not worthwhile. I had to change my way of thinking and relearn how to value myself according to God's Word.

I learned how to process my own pain and change my twisted thinking through the Word of God, one by one, by examining which voices to resist and which voices to accept. That was a long process and there were lots of things that I had to learn. It had to be done in order for me to recover from depression and spiritual oppression.

I eventually learned to value myself and my life because of the Word of God. God values everyone so I need to value everyone. That was very helpful in my healing process from despair and helpless and hopeless thoughts.

6. The Recovery

There were lots of issues that I had to resolve such as anger, forgiveness and despair that I held onto for so long. After I started gaining control of my thoughts and learned to resist the devil's voice and obey the Lord, I experienced healing that I didn't think was possible.

Eventually, with the help of God and the Holy Spirit's healing power, I rose from the pit of depression and came out stronger emotionally, mentally and spiritually. After I was healed, I didn't see demons in other people's faces. Also, I didn't feel beaten by the devil to the point of exhaustion. I came out strong in this process and believe that people who suffer from depression can be healed.

7. Delayed Healing

My healing from depression was a long slow process. I believe my healing would have come sooner if I had the spiritual knowledge of how to overcome depression. As I reflect, there were five reasons why my healing was delayed and lasted more than a year:

(1) Pain – No one explained to me that I needed to take care of my hurts and pain immediately. I kept piling up all my hurts and pain which clogged my mind and caused me emotional, mental and spiritual anguish. It would have been very helpful for me if someone told me to take care of my hurts and pain with God's Word.

After I started reading the Bible, I started processing my problems one by one. It was a lonely and painful process. I didn't know where I was going and how long I had to suffer from depression.

With God's help, I was able to process my grief and loss caused by my sister's death. I was able to let my sister go when I came to believe that she was in heaven with God.

Still, there were many unresolved issues at home. That was one of the reasons why my recovery from depression was slow. After I got married and left home, I was able to let go of much anger and resentment. Again, that healing was delayed after my father's death when I had to forgive him. I was angry that he committed suicide. Eventually, God helped me forgive him.

(2) Destructive Voices – If anyone had warned me that my wrong thinking caused by the spirit of despair could be cured by the Word of God, I would have experienced healing sooner. I attended church all my life

but didn't hear anything about how the devil can plant the seed of twisted thinking in my mind and that it could immobilize me if I accepted it. Also, I didn't know that the Bible had answers for gaining clear thoughts and overcoming a foggy mind.

(3) Spiritual Oppression – I had no knowledge about spiritual oppression and that a person could suffer day and night by tormenting spirits. The reason I knew it was tormenting spirit is because I felt demonic attacks from some people who were working with the devil.

I didn't know how to fight, but the Word of God taught me how. As my faith in Jesus grew, I was able to rebuke the devil. I was able to find spiritual freedom. Jesus said, *"I have given you authority to trample on snakes and scorpions and to overcome all the power of the enemy; nothing will harm you." (Luke 10:19)*

(4) Sin – I didn't realize the power of sin in my life. I learned that as long as I lived in sin and held onto ungodly lifestyle, I would be allowing the devil to attack me. My upbringing, culture, societal values and the abuse at home affected my values and lifestyle which was against God's values. I had to change my attitudes and lifestyle, so I could focus on the Lord and not rely on my own wisdom and understanding.

One of my sins was working with the spirit of worry and fear for so long. I worried and feared for the future and tried to work towards security on my own, which didn't work but brought so much emotional, mental and financial turmoil.

From time to time, I noticed that whenever I start trusting in things or people, the spirit of worry and fear would immobilize me. When Jesus came, he came to destroy the devil's work. Jesus delivered me from the spirit of worry and fear. He came so I can have an abundant life.

"I have come that they may have life, and have it to the full." (John 10:10b)

I learned that if I put people and things above the Lord, then I will become a prisoner of worry and fear. I need to trust my Lord Jesus more than I trust people and things. I need to meditate on the Word of God more than I meditate on worry or fear. I need to be proactive planting positive thoughts from the Word of God so I don't give the devil time to distract me with worries and fear.

There is no peace until I learn to trust in God for all my needs. It took me a long time to trust and have faith in Jesus. I didn't see any hope in life. When God planted hope through the Word of God, I was delivered from despair and depression.

I had to learn that when I am operating on worry and fear, I needed to repent and trust in the Lord. I know what will happen if I listen to the spirit of worry and fear. I will fall back into depression, be immobilized with fear, and overwhelmed with worry. To win this spiritual battle, I have to rely on God's grace and rely on the Word of God. So, I started proclaiming victory in Christ and that helped me to have a proper perspective.

(5) Lack of Purpose – I didn't understand that my purpose in life should be first loving and second serving Jesus. I always believed in Jesus and what He had done for me. For a long time, I had no clue what I should do to have a close relationship with Jesus and what I should do with my life.

Therefore, I made all the plans and I didn't think about what He wanted me to do with my life. That's when I felt something was missing. I kept searching. As I was reading the Bible I realized that I needed to give my life to Jesus and serve Him. Actually, the knowledge that my life was not mine but the Lord's helped me out of my depression. Since then, I have been active in church and have started Bible studies.

It was a painful process going through depression to learn these lessons. But I came out strong and grew in faith because Jesus freed me from depression and gave me a passion for life. *"To the Jews who had believed him, Jesus said, 'If you hold to my teaching, you are really my disciples. Then you will know the truth, and the truth will set you free.'" (John 8:31-32)*

8. The Voice

Even though I no longer suffered from depression, I learned that unless I learned how to deal with different spirits that tried to oppress me, I could fall into depression again.

Whenever I lose focus on the Lord and become consumed with problems in life, the devil tries to trick me to fall into the sin of worry, fear, and despair.

One day I was so stressed out with many challenging issues. While I was driving, I was feeling overwhelmed with the struggles I had. I suddenly heard a voice in my mind telling me to run into a car and kill myself, then my problems would end.

I couldn't believe what I had heard. I immediately recognized where the voice came from. It was the devil's voice trying to commit sin. I rebuked the devil and turned to God for help, and He protected me from the devil's lies. I was glad that I was able to recognize a spiritual battle going on in my mind and was able to resist the twisted thinking.

Having problems in life is not a good enough reason to commit self-murder. If I ran into another car, not only could I kill myself but I could kill or injure others. It would grieve my family and God. The devil was trying to make me focus only on my problems and solving them in the worst way possible.

I was thankful that I knew where this voice came from. I had faith in God that He would help me solve my problems, and He did. Even though I had a difficult childhood, I never had any desire or plans to kill or hurt myself. The devil can use stressful situations to make us fall into sin to hurt not only ourselves but other people.

Having the knowledge that our mind is a spiritual battlefield where the devil speaks to people to tempt them into sin helps me resist destructive thoughts that come to my mind. That's how I found spiritual freedom.

9. Repentance

The spiritual war is going on in our minds every day. One area the devil has tried hard to immobilize me with pain and depressed thoughts is in the area of anger and forgiveness. If I gave in, I would have been in a spiritual prison of depression and turmoil.

Forgiveness is something I had to learn in my spiritual journey if I were to be freed from emotional and spiritual pain. I learned the power of blessing when I was hurt by a woman and had a difficult time forgiving her. I was focusing on her hurtful behaviors and that hurt me more than anything.

Soon, I couldn't think of anything but was overwhelmed with negative thoughts about her. I finally realized what was happening. I had to forgive her, and I tried, but it seemed as though something was holding me back. Then I remembered that Jesus told us to pray and bless our enemies.

After that, whenever I thought about her, I prayed and blessed her. Then the Lord gave me peace and I was able to forgive her. A couple of days later I started blessing this woman, I had a vision of her standing in a beautiful white dress. She had flowers in her hair and was smiling beautifully. She was so beautiful in that vision and God told me I should see others as God sees them – beautiful. I was thankful that God taught me how to bless when I get hurt. Whenever someone hurts me, I say to myself, "I have one more person to bless."

An unforgiving heart opens the door for a spiritual attack. Another time I had a difficult time forgiving someone and I was so filled with anger, disappointment, and sadness. I was flooded with tears. I never cried that much in my life. Tears streamed down my cheeks and I just couldn't stop them. I had no intention of stopping them because I was so upset.

Suddenly, I heard a screaming voice from behind my back. It was the voice of the person who had hurt me. There was no one behind me. I immediately knew what was happening. The devil was screaming at me to scare me with the voice of the person that I had a problem with.

I heard the devil's voice in a dream before and I knew what it sounded like. However, this was the first time I heard the devil's voice in daylight. I could have panicked and thought I am losing my mind if I hadn't understood the devil's tricks. I knew what it was. The devil wanted to make me more upset and angry at the person who had hurt me, so I would focus on hurts and pain and stay in a prison of sadness and anger.

I knew what I had to do right then. I was on my knees, praying. I asked God for forgiveness and I forgave the person who had hurt me. I told God that I bless the person. That stopped my tears, and I found peace. I learned that I needed to take care of any resentment, bitterness and anger right away. Otherwise, it opens the door for the devil to hurt me more.

If I didn't know where that voice was coming from, I

would have been in a prison of bitterness and tormented by demons. I am thankful that God taught me how to forgive so I can be free from spiritual prison.

<u>10. Blessings</u>

I was healed from depression about 35 years ago. Since then I have learned many lessons that keep me from going back to depression. The Word of God helped me to focus on the Lord. I have not been depressed again.

That doesn't mean that the spirit of despair does not attack me anymore. Whenever there is a chance, the spirit of despair tries to make me feel that life is not worthwhile. I know the devil's tricks and spiritual oppression.

I am thankful that God taught me how to resist them with God's Word. To defeat the enemy, I need to know what I am fighting against. The same demons tried to immobilize me with pain and torment when I was depressed and have been trying hard to capture me all my life.

In my spiritual journey of healing, I learned an important lesson of recognizing the voice of God and the voice of the devil. When I hear the voice of despair whispering in my mind, I immediately resist it and say, "I know what's going on. I am not going to accept this lie from the spirit of despair. I know what will happen to me if I accept it. I will fall into depression, a foggy mind and spiritual torment. So, I am going to praise the Lord and think about how I am going to love the Lord and serve Him. I need to focus on how to help others who are in need of healing from God. I decided to pray and raise the number of people that I would like to bring to Christ whenever I feel the devil's attack."

I learned to proclaim victory in Christ that I will be able to use my gifts to the maximum to help others and to save many people. I thank God that I have control over my thoughts, mind and life. I am not going to let the demon to torment me or distract me from loving and serving the Lord.

Loving the Lord has become my first priority. If I love God more than anything or anyone else, I will be able to walk with God. There will be no room for depression when I am trying to love and serve the Lord.

In 1999, God led me to prison ministry. Going into the ministry was one of the best things that happened to me. I have found new motivation to move forward with life and have found clear direction. I have been blessed.

After I started ministry, I became more aware that many people suffer from depression caused by confusing thoughts and spiritual oppression. I am glad that God helped me to see many miracles in my ministry. Healing from depression is one of them. Many people who suffer from depression have learned to rely on the Lord and the Word of God for healing. That's God's grace.

About four years ago, I was reading the Bible and God pointed out that Luke 4:18-19 wasn't just for Jesus but it was for me and for all believers. It says, *"The Spirit of the Lord is on me, because he has anointed me to preach good news to the poor. He has sent me to proclaim freedom for the prisoners and recovery of sight for the blind, to release the oppressed, to proclaim the year of the Lord's favor."*

I am thankful that Jesus is helping people. He certainly helped and changed my life and many others that I have met in my ministry. I am so grateful for that.

Chapter 4

A Pinch of Faith

1. "A PINCH OF FAITH" by Kelly Miller

I started taking anti-depressants when I was 25 years old. At that time I didn't have God in my life. I was going through a divorce and had just been diagnosed with systemic Lupus. Along with all the other medications I was prescribed for Lupus I decided I needed an anti-depressant which was prescribed by my regular family physician.

When I was 31, I had been taking the same anti-depressant for 6 years and was taking the maximum recommended dosage. I needed something stronger. I finally went and was screened by a psychiatrist and officially diagnosed with acute clinical depression. I continued to take many different anti-depressants for the next 12 years, never finding one I felt was working.

In December of 2008, my second husband informed me that he wanted a divorce. For that reason and many more I went on a drinking binge that landed me in ACDF with an F2-second degree felony assault on an officer which carried a mandatory 4 to 12 years prison sentence.

When I went to advisals at the court house, after applying for a public defender, I was taken back to the holding cell where God had an angel waiting for me. I was so upset. She asked if I needed a prayer and I thought, it can't hurt. She asked me if I had accepted Christ as my Savior. I said I had not and told her that I would like to because I had heard all that was needed was the smallest bit of faith, and I knew that, after doing things my way my entire life and getting nowhere. It was time to give God a chance.

I was 41 years old and needed something different. Barbara prayed with me and I know in my heart she was an angel. When I prayed with her and accepted Jesus Christ as my Savior, I experienced the most awesome and unbelievable mental and physical sensation ever. I was surrounded with the presence of warmth pouring over and around my body, and my heart felt swollen with pride and happiness. I can't describe it, but my mind was at ease. When court came, my charges were dropped to an F6-still felony assault. However, I only received 18 months probation in the CESE program. I had been in jail two months, and when I got out my husband had moved on, leaving me literally on the streets. He had either given away, thrown away or kept everything of mine, even my children's pictures and baby books.

I was on the streets because I could not find a home. So, I wasn't compliant and quit going to see my probation officer. I was no longer getting my meds for free. I had to wean myself off anti-depressants after 18 years. Through all this I kept my pinch of faith and kept praying for God's will to be done and not mine. My probation officer issued a warrant that finally caught up with me in August of 2010. I returned to ACDF on violation of probation. By the time I went to sentencing (I was told I would get community corrections) I was so worn out and knew that I was going to end up in a revolving door for many years to come.

I had prayed and prayed prior to sentencing and I wrote a letter to the judge begging for leniency and was sentenced to 30 days in addition to the 60 days I served waiting for court. He also recognized the 16 months out of 18 months that I completed successfully my probation.

I give all the glory to God because I believe it is only because of His mercy and grace that I made it through this, the divorce, probation, losing everything and living on the streets. I am still here, off anti-depressants, getting out of jail a free woman, getting married and best of all, I now have a relationship with God by and through Jesus Christ.

God has helped me with my depression by always being there to listen, putting people and situations in my path to help me and by answering my prayers, of course not in my time but in his time. When I accepted Christ as my Savior and experienced the Holy Spirit, I had renewed hope for my future and a desire to live.

2. "A WAKE UP CALL" by Raelyissa Angelino Garnica

I am almost 30 years old. I'm not one of these kids who came from a bad or broken home. My childhood was very good, and both parents spoiled me. In my early teen years I began running away and getting into trouble. When I was 16 years old, I got knocked up with my son Domenick. He was born at 26 weeks, weighing 2 pounds 11 ounce. He has had about nine surgeries. His dad went to prison for reckless manslaughter when I was 2 months along. Luckily I wasn't alone. I ended up with a good guy named Rick. He cut my son's umbilical cord and raised him like his own from birth. Eleven months later I had my second baby, Alexzandria, who was also a preemie with medical complications. So, here I am, seventeen years old with two kids.

I stayed with Rick for 12 years. Six years into our relationship we had our last baby, Adrian, who was born sick. I never was into drinking or drugs and neither was Rick. We bought our dream house, a 360k home in Reunion. I drove a Chrysler 300 and I owned my own business, "BubbleGum Blast Kids Center."

In 2006 we planned our dream wedding. To the outside we looked envious, but behind closed doors we fought all the time. Six days before our wedding, let's just say it was cancelled. He went to jail. Yet I still stayed with him for two more years. In 2008, we split up. In a matter of months I lost it all! My business closed, my car was repossessed, my home foreclosed and Rick got custody and took my kids.

I was homeless with a bag of clothes and three boxes of pictures, memories, and my kids baby boxes. A so called friend let me stay with her and put my stuff in her storage. She stole about $2,000 from me and went to New Mexico; yes, I lost my stuff, my kids memories and again I was homeless with nothing.

I thought I was so low it was impossible to get back up. Even a little was too hard. I think I was shocked, thinking it could never happen to me. After that, I entered into severe depression. I didn't have my kids, they weren't coming back. So, to get my mind off of them and my problems, I turned to social drinking on weekends with my friends. I found a new crowd and went from never doing drugs or drinking to drinking almost every weekend. It made me forget and helped pass time. Drinking just clouded my thinking and made things so much worse. I was so overwhelmed with my life I gave up and let it be controlled by the influences of other people and their opinions and drinking. I gave Satan control of my life without even knowing it. Look where that got me! In jail and depressed along with everything else.

Coming to jail was a God send. As miserable as it is, it's what I needed. I lost it all – cars, my home, my kids and now my freedom. One night in jail another inmate gave me the book, <u>Journey With Jesus</u>. I said, "I'm not gonna get into God just because I'm in jail." But I got bored with nothing else to do so I read it.

Then, after I started reading a book, <u>*Dancing in the*</u>

Sky, I was touched by an angel. Tears rolled down my face as I read about Chaplain McDonald's loss of her husband, Keith, to a car accident. Something inside felt different as the day went on. I noticed myself changing. I was really reading two books a day and going to a lot of Bible studies.

The next morning, Halloween day, I was still sad. The Chaplain came in with a smile on her face that warmed my soul. We prayed in a group and she gave me some papers of her book to edit. I went back to my cell and thanked God for giving me something to do to pass time.

As I began reading I realized God sent this book to me. Not only to edit it but to read it at this exact moment in my life when I was severely depressed and needed it the most. Everything I was going through was in this *Twisted Logic, The Window of Depression* book. I knew I was meant to read it.

Two days later the Chaplain came back, got the work, and gave me another book to edit. Again we prayed but this time we talked and I told her my story. She invited me to write my story for her future books. I knew she was the sign I asked for.

Now I have a new look at it with God by my side. Here's what I have already gained and I know I have a lifetime more to come. God, Jesus and faith to start I gained knowledge that God took me from my materialist lifestyle and through all that to free me from self glorification, all the no good fake people who were in my life, all the negative. He saved me!

Being in jail isolated me from everyone and everything good and bad, even my kids. At first, and at times, I blamed God and was angry with Him, telling Him, "How could you do this to my kids? They suffered more than enough!" It was to show me how precious they are. I already knew, but He opened my eyes to so much more.

Trusting in Jesus is all I need. He will provide for me all I need in this life. I know now it's not about what I have or do not have. I am still a work in progress and have so much to learn. But this I know the things and life I used to want or had is over, and the new life I am starting is totally opposite. I just want to be humble and live a simple basic life with my kids. I am looking forward to a new life and journey with my kids and with the Lord.

In just 45 days I can feel His power cleaning my soul, changing me every day a little bit more. It's like climbing a mountain the more I get to know Him, the farther I get to the top and the farther Satan flees from me! I am no longer lost. Finding my relationship with the Lord has helped me find myself, my purpose and my future. The Journey With Jesus book and my own journey with Jesus not only changed my life, it saved my life.

3. "ALL YOU NEED IS FAITH" by Cassidy Watkins

I was clinically depressed for 16 years. I was waking up with the feeling of my insides tossed about, complete agony, and suffering so great that I was lost in complete and utter darkness. The devil sat by me constantly. I did not realize that God was still there, for I was blinded by evil and great torment.

The depression started when I was about nine or ten years old. I had been abused physically, mentally by my step-dad and also sexually by an ex-boyfriend of my mom's. My step-dad beat my spirit down severely and my pain only deepened when my mom never left him and is still with him till this day. She even justified the abuse, making it seem as though I deserved it. We were forced to tell my step-dad that we loved him and had to call him dad.

When I got older I rebelled, I called him by his name and no longer pretended to love him. It's because of this that I think my mother has turned on me even more and till this day refuses to protect me. She lives in complete denial to the reality of what his actions did to me. I suffer from PTSD and was suffering from severe depression and panic attacks due to the abuse and the feeling of abandonment from my mother and real father.

I was taking prescription meds thinking they would save me. At the time I could not see that they were actually making me worse. I was constantly having suicidal ideations. Every morning I would awake and dream of dying. I did not realize I was already dead and in hell because I did not accept that what I needed was God to save me and bring me back to life, a life with contentment.

When I was incarcerated, the Holy Spirit found me, (mercy). I began to pray, and I was enlightened to get off my anti-depressant medication. Weeks later, my suffering stopped completely. It was God's healing I needed all along. The balance I needed was from God, not chemicals.

I began to pray and found hope in what God can do; there are no limits. God is infinite (boundless). All I need is faith. God will grant what is good. I had a glimpse of the world of highest happiness (heaven) in a vision.

I would have never had my vision of heaven if I hadn't changed my wicked perceptions. I had vowed to always respect my parents even though they are not here for me. I also vowed not to ever inflict injury on myself or others, whether it be physical or mental pain. Thirdly, I let go of myself completely, knowing and truly believing that everything in this world is temporary.

In meditation on these beliefs one night, all of a sudden I could not feel my body and was at complete peace. I saw a small river in front of me, the sand of the river was like millions of small diamonds. The grains were of all different kinds of colors, flickering, and emitting colorful rays. The water was so beautiful and sparkled like nothing in this world. I could hear the water running peacefully.

I never, not even in my dreams, have been so soothed. I could not stop crying for I was so happy. The tears of joy would not cease. I could see flowers falling from the sky gracefully. Lotus flowers drifted upon the river, the river moving up and down very peacefully and slowly. I could see a golden path. The rest of the ground around it was made of many different colored lights coming from tiny specs, the specs being like neon diamonds. The ground was like looking through the clearest glass I've ever seen. I could see far down into this amazing beautiful ground.

I felt warm and cool breezes. Nothing mattered anymore. I was in so much joy that I had no thoughts of the world I left behind, or anyone, or anything in it. I could not see myself or my body, I was like a mist. Everything was bright with light that does not exist in this world. The light in that world comforts you and is not blinding. It's almost kind of cloudy, like a mist, tiny pieces of what looked like cotton from the cotton trees flowing freely in the air. This place was beyond euphoric in sight and sensation. There was a bright tree close to the river, with huge green leaves, shaped almost like hearts.

Then I came back to myself. I was still sitting on my bunk, in an extreme amount of tears. I could not believe where I had just come from and that it was real! My hands would not stop shaking. I was in so much happiness and shock. I will always do my best to do what is right because that place is well worth it. I can't even put into words how much it is worth. I had been praying every night for God to open my heart and mind. And He did. He opened my mind, body, and soul way more than I could have ever imagined. My vision as to opening my heart was so small compared to His.

I pray every night and then meditate in hopes of returning back to that land. I have no fear of death to this body. In fact I am now anticipating death in this life so that I can be born in the next. And to think there were times in my life that I thought God didn't exist. Wow! I was so wrong. All you need is faith and to let go of the old so that the new can come. Our spirits live forever.

I am so blessed to know what I now know. God showed such mercy on my once lost soul. I believe that anyone can go to heaven, just free yourself from yourself and believe in God! And don't let the devil ever punk (enslave) you. Always look at the reality of things including the reality of your own perceptions. Know that all the good we do will pay off! Heaven is real! Without pain, there cannot be happiness. A flower cannot exist without dirt. Without war I would have not known the value of peace. I believe in cause and effect. It is true what the Bible says, "Love your neighbors because when you hurt them in the end, it will come back on you and you are the one that suffers." Forgiveness and love are the most important things to attain for happiness. Being punished for doing right is more honorable than being punished for doing wrong.

Always thank the Lord. Don't forget what you have received. He highly appreciates your acknowledgement of His work. Appreciation of Him is key. This will bring you closer to Him. And know that He will return His appreciation for you. Don't ever think that He is ignoring your prayers. The prayers that go unanswered are the ones that in the end are not good or right or just have not come yet. Remember God knows best and will only grant what is good.

Chapter 5

Spiritual Counseling for the Depressed Minds

Many people who are depressed have been piling up many emotional, mental, and spiritual issues. That's one of the reasons they feel overwhelmed and immobilized. The following stories are from people who are learning to process their emotional and spiritual pain.

Many of them have a long history of depression. They are still on the journey of healing because it takes time to process their pain. Their stories of how they experience healing in different areas gives others hope, encouragement and direction especially those who suffer from depression.

1. Guilt

I encounter many people who are depressed, that are angry and cannot forgive themselves or others. Their thoughts are consumed with either what other people did wrong or what they did wrong. The pain these people are going through is tremendous to the point that some think it will be better if they commit suicide.

Many people who cannot forgive suffer from twisted thinking which is against the Word of God. God forgives us when we ask for forgiveness, but some people think they shouldn't forgive themselves or they don't deserve to live because they are bad. That goes against God's intention to forgive and cleanse us.

I met a woman who was sober for many years and then she relapsed and suffered from tremendous guilt. She couldn't forgive herself. She thought she didn't deserve to live and asked God to take her life. That lasted many years.

When I met her, she was still struggling from tremendous guilt. I shared that Jesus died for us, and when we ask the Lord for forgiveness, He not only forgives, but forgets our sins as well.

"If we confess our sins, he is faithful and just and will forgive us our sins and purify us from all unrighteousness." (1 John 1:9) *"For I will forgive their wickedness and will remember their sins no more."* (Hebrews 8:12)

Many times when we fail God, ourselves and others, the spirit of despair tries to plant the seed of despair and an unforgiving spirit in our hearts. In her case, she couldn't believe what the Word of God said. She was overwhelmed with guilt, and the devil kept reminding her of her mistakes.

One day God intervened by telling her that He had already forgiven her and she should forgive herself. Since then she is focusing on God's love instead of her mistakes, finding meaning and purpose in life and has been delivered from the spirit of despair.

<u>2. The Pain</u>

I met a young man who broke down in tears and said he couldn't forgive himself for hurting his family. It would be better for him to kill himself so he wouldn't have to hurt his family anymore.

I told him his logic was twisted. His logic was 1+1=5. His twisted logic was that he was hurting his family so if he kills himself, it will be better for his family. But what he didn't realize is that killing himself would hurt his family more than ever. I asked him to listen to his logic and his logic wasn't God's logic.

He needed to develop logical thinking on this issue. He hurt his family so he needs to take care of himself and not get into any more trouble so he can take care of his family. This is 1+1=2.

I told him God is the one who owns his body. Jesus bought him with a price so he should take care of his body and not commit suicide. I asked him to read the Bible to understand who he is in Christ and learn to forgive himself. The second time I met him, he told me that he was feeling better. He finally understood how he should value his life. He told me his body was God's property because He created him. He is the manager of his body and not the owner. He is only taking care of his body for God. Therefore, he cannot destroy God's property.

He was smiling and told me that he knew God was the only one who could give him peace. He started reading the Bible more and growing in the Lord. He told me he was ready to deal with his consequences of failure and had confidence that God was going to help him. I was very glad to hear that.

"Do you not know that your body is a temple of the Holy Spirit, who is in you, whom you have received from God? You are not your own; you were bought at a price. Therefore honor God with your body." (1 Corinthians 6:19-20) "What, then, shall we say in response to this? If God is for us, who can be against us? He who did not spare his own Son, but gave him up for us all--how will he not also, along with him, graciously give us all things?" (Romans 8:31-32)

3. Sadness

Sadness can be caused by an unforgiving spirit. Many people who are depressed suffer from this. Once a woman told me that she was reading the Bible and praying, but she felt sad all the time. As I listened to her, I learned she had lost many important people in her life.

I told her she was grieving and she needs to take care of many emotions that are related to grieving. I explained that when you grieve, you are in a grieving house, and that house has many rooms with different names like guilt, self-pity, anger, regret, forgiveness, blame, isolation and many other emotions.

She told me she finally understood what she needed to do. She needed to work on forgiveness. She was happy to find out what she needed to work on.

When we sin, we cannot have joy. Unforgiveness is sin and we need to take care of it in order to find peace with God, ourselves and others. This doesn't mean that we need to stay in abusive relationships, but we need to take care of our resentments and anger so we can see things clearly, make the right decisions and maintain a good relationship with God who forgives us and fills our hearts with peace and joy.

Jesus said, *"For if you forgive men when they sin against you, your heavenly Father will also forgive you. But if you do not forgive men their sins, your Father will not forgive your sins." (Matthew 6:14-15)*

4. Despair

A man who was in medical unit and hurting badly told me that everyone was after him to kill him. He said he figured out what is going to happen in life. Someone will try to hurt him again, bad things will happen to him today, will happen tomorrow and his life is doomed.

I asked, "Are you a Christian?"

He replied, "Yes."

I said, "You must have gone through a lot of difficulties. But what does God's Word say about all this? What did Jesus say about life? Jesus said, *'The thief comes only to steal and kill and destroy; I have come that they may have life, and have it to the full.' (John 10:10)* Where is this life Jesus is talking about if you are a Christian?"

He didn't have any answer for that. When I asked

him if he was suicidal, he said he wasn't. I asked him to read the Bible and my book, Twisted Logic, The Shadow of Suicide, and tell me what he thought about it.

The next time I met him, he said, "I didn't realize how much I was affected by the spirit of despair for so many years. After I read the book, Twisted Logic, it became clear to me that I need to change my way of thinking. In fact, I tried to commit suicide when I was 18 years old and I didn't realize that I had been this way for so long."

Recognizing what kind of spirit you are dealing with is important. If you want to win a spiritual battle, you also need to know the Word of God and believe in it. That's the first step of healing.

I asked, "Have you ever heard God's voice?"

"How can I hear God's voice? I want to learn how," he replied.

I said, "You need to read the Bible and start processing different areas of hurts and pain. Also, ask God for forgiveness and let go of anger and bitterness. Then, practice listening to God's voice in silence. Ask the Lord to speak to you and wait in silence. When God speaks to you, you will recognize it. He might tell you through the Word of God or He might want to speak to you and tell you some things you need to hear. The Holy Spirit can guide, direct, comfort, and let you know what is going to happen in the future through dreams and through words. You need to pay attention to the thoughts that come to your mind. There are four voices: Other people's voices; your voice; the devil's voice and the Holy Spirit's voice. You need to resist any destructive thoughts which come from the devil. You need to obey the Holy Spirit when He asks you to do things so you can grow and help others grow in faith."

I also asked him if he knew his calling.

He replied, "No."

I said, "Each one of us has a calling. You can start asking God what your calling is." I also told him that when he starts recognizing God's voice, his calling will become clear to him. God has plans for him and he needs to spend time with the Word of God to understand what he should do with his life.

We are to love the Lord and serve the Lord. Love our neighbors is serving the Lord. How can we do it? We are to be Jesus' witness and to make disciples. I told him how Jesus gave us direction, but how he uses his gifts to obey the Lord is up to him. *"Then Jesus came to them and said, 'All authority in heaven and on earth has been given to me. Therefore go and make disciples of all nations, baptizing them in the name of the Father and of the Son and of the Holy Spirit, and teaching them to obey everything I have commanded you. And surely I am with you always, to the very end of the age.'" (Matthew 28:18-20)*

5. Grief and Anger

I once visited a woman in suicide observation and she was deeply troubled.

"I have been in depression and had a lot of counseling, but nothing is getting any better. In fact, I am in so much pain that no one is able to help me."

I asked her if she believed in God, and she said yes. Then she told me that she took many different anti-depressant medications and they weren't working. To ease her pain she started using drugs, and in the process, she lost everything, even freedom and self-respect.

I asked, "You weren't like this before, is that right?"

"No, there were a lot of good times, and I never used the drugs to numb my pain."

"When was the last time that you were functioning normal and had a good life?"

"About three years ago," she replied.

"What was it that caused all this pain and caused you to start using drugs? Something happened and made your life change. What was it?" I asked.

"It was when my husband shot himself in front of me. I loved him, and since his death I have gotten into so much trouble. Now, I feel like my life is not worthwhile. I hurt so many people, including my children."

"I know what you need to do. You need to process grief. You are stuck in a grief room. You need to process many areas, like anger, resentment, forgiveness, blame, letting him go and many other emotions."

She broke down in tears and said, "I knew there was something wrong with me. Why didn't anybody tell me this before. You are the first one who is telling me that I need to take care of my grief. For so long, others tried to give me medication and never told me that my husband's death was affecting me and I needed to take care of it. This makes sense."

"Many people don't know how to deal with grief and loss and they are stuck in pain. It could lead them to depression if they don't take care of it. I know this because I too was stuck in a grief room more than once. Until I processed my grief with God's help, I wasn't able to function normally."

"I have a difficult time forgiving my husband and I haven't let him go. I love him, so I was holding on to him."

"Those are the areas that you need to work on forgiveness and letting him go." Since she was in suicide observation, she couldn't have any books. I told her after she is discharged she should read my book, *Dancing in the Sky,* so she can learn how to process grief. I told her that until she takes care of the grief and the loss of her husband, she cannot be released from pain and suffering.

I told her the lesson of gifts in life. Her husband was

a temporary gift and God understands her grief and pain and He can help her. Everything is a temporary gift from the Lord: our family, material things, jobs, ministry and even our own life. That being said, we need to treat them as temporary gifts. Otherwise, we will be so lost when we lose them. I was lost when I lost my husband and immobilized with pain, even though I had faith in God.

One of the greatest lessons I learned from my husband's death was the lesson that we don't own anything. God owns everything. I was going to grieve for the rest of my life and God pointed out that in order for me to experience healing, I have to let my husband go. Until I let my husband go, I suffered so much and was immobilized.

So one day I prayed to the Lord, "Please help me deal with my loss of Keith."

God replied, "My daughter, it wasn't a loss. He wasn't yours anyway. He is mine, my child, no one else can claim him as theirs. Nothing you have is yours; it is all mine. Everything you have is a temporary gift. When you know what you truly own, you will be healed from any distractions. You are a temporary keeper and manager of your house and furniture and everything else in it. You don't own your children. They are mine, also."

I answered, "Thank you, Lord, for helping me realize that." Within three months, I was not grieving because I processed all the areas related to grief and pain. God told me to let go of my husband if I wanted healing from grief and pain, so I did. After that I didn't grieve anymore.

Before I left, I prayed for the healing of her mind from the trauma that she suffered seeing her husband's traumatic death and also for healing from grief and loss.

She followed my suggestion. After she was

discharged from the suicide observation unit, she started reading the book _Dancing in the Sky_. Within a week, I met her in the housing unit. I saw a smile on her face for the first time.

I knew she had a transformation and a breakthrough in her grieving process. She stopped me and thanked me for helping her to process her grief and loss. She told me that she was finally able to let go of her husband and was on the road to recovery.

She told me that she still had many other issues she had to work on but this was the beginning of her new life. She can move on instead of being stuck in pain and grief. She understood that people who are in grief are self-absorbed and cannot understand other's pain.

After she experienced healing, she was able to see that her family needed her, and she needed to take care of her children who need healing caused by her drug addiction and loss of their father from suicide.

6. Spiritual Deliverance

One day as I was in a housing unit and an inmate who looked disturbed approached me. She told me that she was having a difficult time. She was hearing voices behind her and seeing things that others did not see. She had a long history of mental problems. She believed in God. She told me medication didn't help her.

I knew that what she needed was spiritual healing. I told her that what happened in Bible times can happen to her. She can experience healing by rebuking the devil in Jesus' name to leave her. She was not convinced. I prayed for her healing but she had to believe for herself that Jesus could free her from spiritual confusion and torment.

She had to grow her faith in Jesus to resist the devil's attacks. I knew she could do it, but she just didn't believe in the spiritual world or that spiritual beings could attack and torment her.

About three months later she stopped me in the housing unit again. This time she was radiant and smiling. I could tell that she had a spiritual breakthrough. She shared with me what had happened.

Since I had talked to her the last time another inmate asked her to attend a worship service. There, people believed the same way I did about her illness. She followed their suggestion and proclaimed Jesus' power and told the devil to leave. Once she did that, she no longer had problems hearing voices or seeing things. Since then she has started attending worship services regularly and prays to Jesus every day.

She became a firm believer that Jesus has the power to heal people. She learned to rely on Jesus and not on other people to resist spiritual influences. Unless the person believes in Jesus' power, it is difficult to restore the person's spiritual health.

She told me that her doctor was surprised to find out that she was healed. She told me she didn't need to take anti-depressant medicine after that.

I don't believe that all mental illness can be cured in this way. Some people have brain damage, and some need medical care. In fact, in many cases, doctors can help restore health.

Some people felt better after they took anti-depressant medicine. I believe the doctors are helping many people who have physical, emotional and mental problems, but in some cases, people need spiritual healing. This was such a case.

This woman attended my Forgiveness class. It was very encouraging for me to see that she was rebuking the demon every day and growing in the Lord. This event gave me more confidence in God who has the power to help us heal our hearts and minds.

"When Jesus had called the Twelve together, he gave them power and authority to drive out all demons and to cure diseases, and he sent them out to preach the kingdom of God and to heal the sick." (Luke 9:1-2)

"I have given you authority to trample on snakes and scorpions and to overcome all the power of the enemy; nothing will harm you." (Luke 10:19)

7. Grief and Hope

A woman suffered from deep depression and Post Traumatic Stress Disorder. This happened while she was in the military. She tried to numb her pain with drugs which led her to jail.

After she lost her father, she was in a considerable amount of emotional and mental pain and stuck in grief. Before he died his legs were amputated and he suffered greatly. She was very close to her father and seeing him suffer before he died broke her heart. She had been crying so long that her grief was consuming her time and energy. She couldn't focus on anything else and was suicidal at some point and immersed in pain.

When I first met her, she asked me which Scripture talked about running and walking and having strength in God. I told her it's in Isaiah chapter 40. I knew then that the Holy Spirit was trying to help her have a bigger picture of her father's death. The Word of God gives us a big picture of eternity, God's plans and helps many grieving people. I believe that's what God was trying to teach her. I told her to work on the different areas she needs to deal with when she grieves, such as blame, anger, forgiveness, grieving, and letting him go through prayer.

The next time I met her, I knew God had opened her heart to see the big picture when I saw her beaming smile.

She said, "That Scripture you told me about was right. It was Isaiah chapter 40. I read it and God brought healing to me. My father couldn't walk on earth when he was alive, but now he is in heaven walking and running. It gives me comfort knowing that he is doing better in heaven than being here. He doesn't suffer any more. I can finally let him go through prayer as you have suggested and it worked. Now I have peace and joy. When my father was alive, he told me to take care of my younger son, and that's what I am going to do."

I was very glad that she found direction and was able to move on. While she was incarcerated, she edited the *Maximum Saints* books which are written by Adams County Detention Facility inmates. She found joy in helping others. For people who feel depressed because of loss and cannot feel any strength, read Isaiah and meditate on it day and night. This woman saw her father walking and running in her mind and experienced healing. You can apply this to anyone who cannot walk or run or are in need of strength.

Here is the Scripture that comforted her: *"Do you not know? Have you not heard? The Lord is the everlasting God, the Creator of the ends of the earth. He will not grow tired or weary, and his understanding no one can fathom. He gives strength to the weary and increases the power of the weak. Even youths grow tired and weary, and young men stumble and fall; but those who hope in the Lord will renew their strength. They will soar on wings like eagles; they will run and not grow weary, they will walk and not be faint." (Isaiah 40:28-31)* Even if some people cannot gain physical strength here on earth, in heaven we have hope of being whole again.

8. Spiritual Confusion

Once I was leading a prayer meeting in a pod. Afterwards we sat and discussed prayer requests in a circle. We heard a woman screaming and yelling in a room. A woman told me, "She has a demon, and we need to pray for her. I hear her screaming all night, and I am so scared to go to sleep." The deputy was already there to help her.

I explained to them that we should pray for her and said, "She doesn't have a demon. She is a Christian and I have talked to her before. You don't need to be scared of the situation. The demon is bothering her. She is probably hearing the voice of a demon and she is fighting back. She probably doesn't know how to handle it. I will try to talk to her later."

The next day, I called her out and asked her what happened. She explained that she had been suffering because of a woman that she couldn't forgive. "I cannot even see the mirror. If I do, instead of seeing my face, I see her face, I hear her voice, and she has been hurting me. I am so angry at her."

I said, "You need to forgive and let go of your anger. The demon knows how much you hate her, so the spirit is talking to you with her voice and showing her face to you in the mirror. That's not her. A human cannot do that. It's the evil spirits trying to make you mad at the woman so you will focus on hate and anger. Did you hear her voice when you were in your room?"

"Yes, she talks to me and I just cannot get rid of her. No one has been able to help me."

"This is what I would suggest you do. The next time you hear any voice, rebuke the demon in Jesus' name to leave. Then don't scream and fight or argue with the demon. Just start to pray and start reading the Bible more, so you can focus on the Lord and not the voices of the demon. You have to learn to focus on Jesus more than hating someone. As we focus on hate and anger, we are opening the door for the devil."

"I cannot believe how much I have been suffering

from this woman."

"It's not the woman who hurt you. It's the demon and you need to learn to forgive, to let it go. I can tell you that one day I was so upset and angry at someone that I cried and cried. I couldn't stop my tears. I was focusing on the person who hurt me. Then suddenly, I heard a screaming voice from behind me, and that voice was the person I was upset with. I knew what it was. It was not a person's voice. It was a demon's voice. I have heard a demon's voice in my dream before. That's how the devil works to make us hate others. I immediately asked God to forgive me for holding resentment. The demon took advantage of the situation by trying to make me angrier at the person. So, it's time to forgive."

"I don't know how to forgive," she said.

"Jesus asked us to love our enemies, pray for them and bless them. You need to obey the Lord in order for you to experience healing from an unforgiving spirit. I had to bless the woman who hurt me. It worked for me, and it will help you as well."

She said she would try to forgive her. It is the beginning of healing. I told her that she should ignore the demon's voice instead of responding to the voice. That's what the devil wants. She should keep reading the Bible so she can grow spiritually. I asked her to process her pain, one by one. Forgiveness is one area that she needs to take care of. The Lord will show her other areas that she needs healing. I told her that God can help her forgive so she needs to ask for forgiveness for holding resentment. I prayed for her healing and God's leadership so she can find peace.

She left the facility not long after that. I asked others in the same pod how was she before she left. They said that somehow she was calm and didn't scream anymore. They said she seemed to have some healing in her heart.

"'In your anger do not sin': Do not let the sun go down while you are still angry, and do not give the devil a foothold." (Ephesians 4:26-27) "See to it that no one misses the grace of God and that no bitter root grows up to cause trouble and defile many." (Hebrews 12:15)

9. The Tormenting Spirit

I emphasize listening to God's voice in worship services. Many people have not learned to pay attention to the Holy Spirit. Instead, many are hurting and are in so much pain. Without realizing it, many people have accepted the devil's lies so they cannot be forgiven.

At one of the chaplain's worship services, I talked about voices we hear and how we should be careful not to accept the devil's tricks. Many times the devil will make a suggestion so we can fall into sin.

If we don't resist it, we might follow the devil's suggestion and fall into sin. After that, the devil will try to beat us down with guilt and shame. After we ask God to forgive us, we are forgiven. But the devil will tell us how worthless and useless we are and God cannot forgive us. We should not beat ourselves down. That's what the devil wants us to do. God brings healing and forgiveness so we can have peace instead of turmoil.

After the worship, a man approached me and said, "What you have spoken to us is just for me. I used to be a Satanist and then became a Christian. I repented but the devil has been telling me that God cannot forgive a person like me. The devil has been after me and I have been struggling with this for so long."

"That's one of the devil's tactics to discourage people. Many people suffer from accusing voices after they repent. You need to fight it with the Scripture."

As we were talking, I felt the devil's attack in my body and I knew the demon who was after him was trying to distract our conversation. I said, "Let's pray. I feel I need to pray for you." I started praying and suddenly, I started coughing, choking, and the words wouldn't come out. I couldn't pray and I was gasping for air. This never happened to me before when I tried to pray for someone.

The man said, "The demon is choking you so you cannot pray for me. Sometimes demons try to choke me like that for more than 24 hours at a time. I know the demon is upset. Now I believe in God. I am still struggling with the demon."

I said, "Well, you need to be strong, keep reading the Bible and praying so you will be strong and the demon cannot bother you. So, I need to pray for you again."

So, I prayed for him and this time I was able to finish the prayer. That was one experience that I will never forget.

The tormenting demon is after so many people, even people who believe in God. When I suffered from depression and was bedridden, I suffered from nightmares. The demon was choking me and I had a difficult time breathing. The nightmares disappeared after I started reading the Bible, prayed and processed lots of hurts and rebuked the demons that tortured me. I believed in God all my life and nothing else, but still the spirit knew I was a spiritual baby and kept attacking me until I grew in the knowledge of the Word of God and learned to resist the devil.

I learned that many who used to be open to Satan and spirits other than God, are more vulnerable to torment by demons than others who continuously walk with God. The demon is angry that these people have now become believers of God. These people become a threat to Satan's work. So, the demons try to discourage them from serving the Lord by attacking and distracting them.

Many are constantly suffering from spiritual attack. At the same time, I have seen many who have grown spiritually after they learned how to fight and win the spiritual battle. Jesus has more power than the devil, so healing and deliverance is possible. When these people finally learn to understand the power of the Holy Spirit and the Word of God, they can have peace knowing that the devil doesn't have power over them. All the devil can do is scare people, but I learned not to be scared. I have faith in the Lord.

In fact, those who have the gift of discernment learn to know the spiritual world and also learn to fight and overcome the devil. Faith in Jesus can help others more than those who have never had spiritual experiences. I feel I have an advantage in that matter because I have experienced the spiritual world and know how to win the battle by relying on God. Jesus has the power, and we need to claim it to win the spiritual battle.

I have heard from many people who have had spiritual eyes and ears opened. Many were scared and I told them, "You don't have to be afraid. You have a gift of spiritual discernment. All you have to do is rely on the Lord Jesus to win the spiritual battles. Start reading the Bible and pray more so you can focus on the Lord. Rebuke the devil in the name of Jesus and start to proclaim victory in Christ. Start asking God to forgive you if you have sinned. When you sin and do not repent, you open the door of your heart to the devil for accusation and your conscience will start bothering you. Moreover, the Holy Spirit will be convicting your sins if you are a child of God. Also, tormenting demons can attack you by telling you that you are a bad person."

The devil cannot beat you with guilt and shame

when you repent. Just remember that there are different voices you hear and you have to reject the devil's voice and resist it by relying on Jesus. After you repent, there is a chance that the devil might try to tell you that God cannot forgive you because you are a bad person. This doesn't come from the Lord but comes from the devil. The Lord Jesus has given us the power and authority to resist the devil. So I know it's possible for you to be healed and come out strong with faith in the Lord. This experience will give you more understanding of the spiritual world. You just need to learn how to overcome it with God's power. The man's face lit up and he said, "Now, I know where those voices are coming from. I was told to hurt others and I need to resist it."

Jesus has the power to help you. You need God's wisdom to handle spiritual battle. Read Ephesians 6:10-20)

John wrote, *"You, dear children, are from God and have overcome them, because the one who is in you is greater than the one who is in the world." (1 John 4:4)* Peter wrote, *"Humble yourselves, therefore, under God's mighty hand, that he may lift you up in due time. Cast all your anxiety on him because he cares for you. Be self-controlled and alert. Your enemy the devil prowls around like a roaring lion looking for someone to devour. Resist him, standing firm in the faith, because you know that your brothers throughout the world are undergoing the same kind of sufferings. And the God of all grace, who called you to his eternal glory in Christ, after you have suffered a little while, will himself restore you and make you strong, firm and steadfast. To him be the power forever and ever. Amen." (1 Peter 5:6-11)*

10. Fear

A woman was suffering from a voice that confused her. As we were talking, suddenly she stopped and said that she heard the voice say that she will go to prison. "Do you think I will go to prison?" she asked.

"Did you do any crime for which the police would be after you?" I asked.

She replied, "No."

"Then you shouldn't believe what you have heard. I believe the devil is trying to plant the seed of fear into your heart. Don't believe it."

I explained to her that there are voices and thoughts that come to our mind that are not ours and are destructive in nature. We need to resist them. One reason she was so confused and couldn't have a clear mind was because the enemy was speaking to her with confusing and twisted words.

I explained to her how to find out what she needs to work on to gain a clear mind and freedom from emotional and spiritual pain. She has to commit to know the Word of God by reading and meditating every day. Also, I told her how to recognize and resist confusing voices and replace them with God's life-giving Words.

If you are deeply depressed, there is a chance that you have accepted destructive voices. Take care of them one by one to find hope through the Word of God. Your healing will depend on how much twisted logic you have accepted and how much you can replace them with the Word of God. That's why you need to know the Bible to resist any wrong thoughts. When you are able to let go of destructive voices in your mind, you will experience a breakthrough and your mind will be clear.

11. The Voice

A woman used to be filled with joy when she read the Bible, and she was comforted. Then when she started having many problems with people and sunk into a deep depression. Then she had a difficult time focusing and suffered from a foggy mind. She stopped reading the Bible because she had a difficult time focusing on the Word of God. Also, when she read the Bible something was twisting the meaning of the Word of God. This had never happened to her before.

"I was reading Revelation where it talks about fallen angels. I was wondering if I was one of them. Do you think I am a fallen angel?"

I knew where it was coming from. The devil was twisting the Word of God to confuse her. She didn't realize that it was the devil. I asked, "Are you an angel?"

"No," she replied.

I said, "You are not an angel. Therefore, you cannot be a fallen angel."

She continued reading the Bible and resisting the devil's voice and twisted interpretation. She finally saw improvement in the control over mind and she prayed more. God blessed her and she heard that she should write a confession letter, so she did.

After she started recognizing God's voice, she found joy. She gained confidence that God was going to help her overcome depression. God continuously spoke to her. One of the things He told her to do is dance for the Lord. She started dancing for the Lord, and this brought great healing in her. Worshipping the Lord brings healing.

12. Bitterness

A woman was deeply depressed. I suggested to her that she start asking God for forgiveness by going back to her early life. The reason for that is many depressed people have not taken care of their past hurts and pains, and they seem to have many mental files in their cabinets that need to be taken care of.

We prayed that the Holy Spirit will help cleanse her heart by repenting. God helped her to repent many things that she had forgotten, and one of the areas she had to take care of was her relationship with her father.

She said, "My mother died when I was young, and my father raised three daughters. He was very strict. In my teen years I got pregnant. I was afraid of my father's rejection and punishment, so I had an abortion. When my older sister got pregnant in her teen years, my father kicked her out of the house and she suffered greatly. I didn't want to go through what she had, so I had an abortion. It affected me greatly. I suffered tremendous guilt and shame. I finally was able to forgive myself. I don't know why this thought came to my mind now, but I think I need to forgive my father and that's why it came up. If he was kinder, I wouldn't have had an abortion. I made that decision out of fear."

"I am glad that you were able to forgive yourself. God knows that you have been carrying resentment for so long and I believe the Holy Spirit has brought this up. It's time to forgive your father. So, let's pray."

She prayed for God's forgiveness for holding resentment against her father for so long and told Him she forgives her father.

About two weeks later, she also shared that God gave her a Scripture to teach her how to think about her father. *"Children, obey your parents in the Lord, for this is right. 'Honor your father and mother'--which is the first commandment with a promise--'that it may go well with you and that you may enjoy long life on the earth.'" (Ephesians 6:1-3)*

She shared that for a long time she focused on her father's strictness and she harbored resentment and bitterness. She prayed and asked God for forgiveness, and she forgave her father.

About a week later, God showed her what she had been lacking in herself through the Scripture: *"Honor your father and your mother, so that you may live long in the land the Lord your God is giving you." (Exodus 20:12)* She learned that she should have been honoring her father by obeying him instead of going against her father's wishes. Her focus now is going beyond resentment or anger. It is focused on restoring her love and respect for her father.

In order for her to continuously develop a good attitude toward her father and have a good memory of him, she needed to change her perception. That's how she was to honor her father and she hadn't been doing that. This Scripture has motivated her to see the things she wasn't able to see before.

Now there is no room for harsh feelings toward her father when she decided to obey the Lord. I told her I was glad that the Holy Spirit has started a deep healing in her. In order for us to forgive, not only do we need to repent and say the words to be healed completely, we have to respect others that deserve respect, and in this case, it was her father.

Reflection

Do you suffer from painful thoughts that come back to you over and over again? That is what you need to process. Sometimes people think they took care of their past painful events but if you have a strong feeling whenever you think about it, you have not completely processed all the emotion that was caused by the event or people. Ask the Lord to help you process your pain. Start reading the Bible. He can heal you from pain and hurts and bring you healing.

Chapter 6

Distressed People's Stories in the Bible

<u>1. Elijah – A prophet who was afraid and wanted to die</u>

The story of Elijah is an example of how a person can be affected by the spirit of worry and fear when they are afraid of people's words instead of relying on God who sent fire from heaven to burn his sacrifice and gave rain when he prayed. He was so terrified that he thought it would be better for him to die.

God, however, had the plan to restore his courage and sent him back to do what he was supposed to do. We can learn from this story that there is hope for those who are distressed and overwhelmed with life and suffer from depression. God had a plan to help Elijah when he was emotionally, mentally and spiritually stressed out.

"Now Ahab told Jezebel everything Elijah had done and how he had killed all the prophets with the sword. So Jezebel sent a messenger to Elijah to say, 'May the gods deal with me, be it ever so severely, if by this time tomorrow I do not make your life like that of one of them.'

Elijah was afraid and ran for his life. When he came to Beersheba in Judah, he left his servant there while he himself went a day journey into the desert. He came to a broom tree, sat down under it and prayed that he might die. 'I have had enough, Lord,' he said. 'Take my life; I am no better than my ancestors.' Then he lay down under the tree and fell asleep.

All at once an angel touched him and said, 'Get up and eat.' He looked around, and there by his head was a cake of bread baked over hot coals, and a jar of water. He ate and drank and then lay down again. The angel of the Lord came back a second time and touched him and said, 'Get up and eat, for the journey is too much for you.' So he got up and ate and drank. Strengthened by that food, he traveled forty days and forty nights until he reached Horeb, the mountain of God.

There he went into a cave and spent the night. And the word of the Lord came to him: 'What are you doing here, Elijah?' He replied, 'I have been very zealous for the Lord God Almighty. The Israelites have rejected your covenant, broken down your altars, and put your prophets to death with the sword. I am the only one left, and now they are trying to kill me too.'

The Lord said, 'Go out and stand on the mountain in the presence of the Lord, for the Lord is about to pass by.' Then a great and powerful wind tore the mountains apart and shattered the rocks before the Lord, but the Lord was not in the wind. After the wind there was an earthquake, but the Lord was not in the earthquake. After the earthquake came a fire, but the Lord was not in the fire.

And after the fire came a gentle whisper. When Elijah heard it, he pulled his cloak over his face and went out and stood at the mouth of the cave.

Then a voice said to him, 'What are you doing here, Elijah?' He replied, 'I have been very zealous for the Lord God Almighty. The Israelites have rejected your covenant, broken down your altars, and put your prophets to death with the sword. I am the only one left, and now they are trying to kill me too.'

The Lord said to him, 'Go back the way you came, and go to the Desert of Damascus. When you get there, anoint Hazael king over Aram.'" (1 kings 19:1-15) "Yet I reserve seven thousand in Israel--all whose knees have not bowed down to Baal and all whose mouths have not kissed him." (1 Kings 19:18)

When Elijah was ready to die from overwhelming fear, God took care of him and gave him the instruction to seek the Lord. That's what we need to do. Elijah followed God's instructions. He focused on finding God instead of being immobilized with fear. He was listening. He heard God's whispering voice. He told Elijah to go back the way he came and anoint a new king. Elijah obeyed the Lord. God told him he was not the only believer in God, but He saved 7,000 people who serve God. Hearing God's voice of instruction on how to serve the Lord will bring healing to our hearts. We are not alone in our distressful times. God wants to help us and listening to His voice is a very important step of recovery from a distressing situations.

Prayer: "Lord, you know my heart. Help me to hear your clear voice and help me to see the big picture that you see so I don't have to be afraid of people or difficult situations. Help me to have the courage to follow you and your plans. Amen."

2. The King Saul – Tormented by spirits

When Saul disobeyed the Lord, and didn't repent and turn to the Lord, he suffered from a tormenting spirit.

"Now the Spirit of the Lord had departed from Saul, and an evil spirit from the Lord tormented him. Saul's attendants said to him, 'See, an evil spirit from God is tormenting you. Let our Lord command his servants here to search for someone who can play the harp. He will play when the evil spirit from God comes upon you, and you will feel better.' So Saul said to his attendants, 'Find someone who plays well and bring him to me.' One of the servants answered, 'I have seen a son of Jesse of Bethlehem who knows how to play the harp. He is a brave man and a warrior. He speaks well and is a fine-looking man. And the Lord is with him.' Then Saul sent messengers to Jesse and said, 'Send me your son David, who is with the sheep.' So Jesse took a donkey loaded with bread, a skin of wine and a young goat and sent them with his son David to Saul. David came to Saul and entered his service. Saul liked him very much, and David became one of his armor-bearers. Then Saul sent word to Jesse, saying, 'Allow David to remain in my service, for I am pleased with him.' Whenever the spirit from God came upon Saul, David would take his harp and play. Then relief would come to Saul; he would feel better, and the evil spirit

would leave him." (1 Samuel 16:14-23)

Even in suffering, Saul didn't turn to the Lord for healing instead he listened to other people's suggestions for a temporary solution. God was with David and his music relieved Saul from tormenting spirits.

This tells us that when we are disobedient and don't turn to the Lord, we can be tormented by spirits. Our sinful desires and actions open the doors for the spirit of torment to hurt us.

Many suffer from deep emotional and spiritual pain and don't have any physical problems. If this happens to you, turn to the Lord and ask for help and start repenting of your sins. We need to continuously walk with God in order to have the spiritual strength to resist the evil spirits.

This story tells us that being around people who are walking with God helps us. We need to surround ourselves with people who fear God for our own well-being. That is why it is important to attend worship services and Bible studies to learn about God and to learn from other mature Christians.

Prayer: "Lord, I ask you to forgive me when I turn to people for a temporary solution. Help me to seek your advice and help me to see myself clearly so I can repent and not grieve. Release me from any evil spirit that is trying to put me in a spiritual prison of torture. Help me to obey you with a willing heart. "

3. Jonah – Distressed in the belly of the fish

Jonah had to learn a great lesson of obedience in his time of distress. The Scripture says, *"The word of the Lord came to Jonah son of Amittai: 'Go to the great city of Nineveh and preach against it, because its wickedness has come up before me.' But Jonah ran away from the Lord and headed for Tarshish. He went down to Joppa, where he found a ship bound for that port. After paying the fare, he went aboard and sailed for Tarshish to flee from the Lord. Then the Lord sent a great wind on the sea, and such a violent storm arose that the ship threatened to break up." (Jonah 1:1-4)*

If Jonah had repented at that spot and obeyed the Lord, he wouldn't have had to go through being swallowed by a fish, and suffer inside the fish for three days. Instead of repenting, Jonah asked the other shipmen to throw him in the sea. He was ready to die instead of being obedient to the Lord. What Jonah didn't realize is that his life is not in his hands but the Lord's, even in the sea. God prepared a fish that would swallow Jonah. Inside the fish, Jonah was in so much distress that he cried out to God for help.

"From inside the fish Jonah prayed to the Lord his God. He said: 'In my distress I called to the Lord, and he answered me. From the depths of the grave I called for help, and you listened to my cry. You hurled me into the deep, into the very heart of the seas, and the currents swirled about me; all your waves and breakers swept over me. I said, 'I have been banished from your sight; yet I will look again toward your holy temple.' The engulfing waters threatened me, the deep surrounded me; seaweed was wrapped around my head. To the roots of the mountains I sank down; the earth beneath barred me in forever. But you brought my life up from the pit, O Lord my God. 'When my life was ebbing away, I remembered you, Lord, and my prayer rose to you, to your holy temple...' And the Lord commanded the fish, and it vomited Jonah onto dry land." (Jonah 2:1-10)

There is suffering and pain caused by natural disasters, as well as our weaknesses and by other person's ungodly behaviors. There are also times we have caused our own pain and suffering. The sad thing is we may not even realize it. We need to look at our situation and see if we have caused our distress and pain through disobedience and an ungodly lifestyle. If we disobey the Lord, it's time to repent and get right with the Lord. Sometimes our troubled times are God trying to get our attention.

Prayer: "Lord Jesus, I feel like I am inside a fish like Jonah. Please save me from my distress and anguish. I ask for your forgiveness if I have sinned against you with my ungodly lifestyle and disobedient heart. I ask for your forgiveness for my family and others who have sinned against you. Have mercy on me, a sinner, and wash me with the blood of Jesus Christ and cleanse me from my sin. Help me to know what is right and wrong and to obey you. I ask you to give me a second chance to obey you as you did with Jonah. I pray that I will be able to love you and obey you."

4. Habakkuk – His leg trembled in fear of disaster

The prophet Habakkuk heard from the Lord that his nation will be invaded by another nation because people turned against the Lord. As Habakkuk was waiting for the disaster to come, he describes how much he was in distress and turmoil and also how he handled his distress.

He wrote, *"I heard and my heart pounded, my lips quivered at the sound; decay crept into my bones, and my legs trembled. Yet I will wait patiently for the day of calamity to come on the nation invading us. Though the fig tree does not bud and there are no grapes on the vines, though the olive crop fails and the fields produce no food, though there are no sheep in the pen and no cattle in the stalls, yet I will rejoice in the Lord, I will be joyful in God my Savior. The Sovereign Lord is my strength; he makes my feet like the feet of a deer, he enables me to go on the heights." (Habakkuk 3:16-19) "Lord, I have heard of your fame; I stand in awe of your deeds, O Lord. Renew them in our day, in our time make them known; in wrath remember mercy." (Habakkuk 3:1)*

Habakkuk understood what God was doing and prayed for mercy for his nation, but at the same time he knew that disaster was coming. He proclaims his faith that he will rejoice in the Lord because God is his strength in times of trouble. In our difficult times, we may see nothing that can give us joy, but we can rejoice in the Lord for what He can do to help us. Sometimes we suffer from our mistakes and sins and sometimes we suffer because of other people's sins. This is not the time to turn away and be angry with the Lord but to turn to Him for mercy. We can learn to rejoice in the Lord even though our circumstances do not make us happy.

Prayer: "Lord, please help me to understand why I am in so much pain and distress. If there is any sin I have committed and I am paying the consequences for, please forgive me and have mercy on me. Release me from this pain and distress. I also ask you to forgive others who have sinned against you. Let me rejoice in you, Lord. Save me from this anguish so I can see your hands carrying me."

5. Nebuchadnezzar – Proud attitude brought disasters

The Scripture says, *"I, King Nebuchadnezzar, To the peoples, nations and men of every language, who live in all the world: May you prosper greatly! It is my pleasure to tell you about the miraculous signs and wonders that the Most High God has performed for me. How great are his signs, how mighty his wonders! His kingdom is an eternal kingdom; his dominion endures from generation to generation." (Daniel 4:1-3)*

The king of Babylon knew God and recognized His greatness and praised Him. The king was prosperous. Then he had a dream that distressed him. *"I, Nebuchadnezzar, was at home in my palace, contented and prosperous. I had a dream that made me afraid. As I was lying in my bed, the images and visions that passed through my mind terrified me." (Daniel 4:4-5)* Daniel interpreted the king's dream and told him to be humble before God and obey Him. Otherwise he will be thrown out of the kingship and would end up eating like a wild animal. *(Daniel 4:19-27)*

The king didn't pay attention to Daniel and he had a

spirit of pride. Daniel wrote, *"All this happened to King Nebuchadnezzar. Twelve months later, as the king was walking on the roof of the royal palace of Babylon, he said, 'Is not this the great Babylon I have built as the royal residence, by my mighty power and for the glory of my majesty?' The words were still on his lips when a voice came from heaven, 'This is what is decreed for you, King Nebuchadnezzar: Your royal authority has been taken from you. You will be driven away from people and will live with the wild animals; you will eat grass like cattle. Seven times will pass by for you until you acknowledge that the Most High is sovereign over the kingdoms of men and gives them to anyone he wishes.' Immediately what had been said about Nebuchadnezzar was fulfilled. He was driven away from people and ate grass like cattle. His body was drenched with the dew of heaven until his hair grew like the feathers of an eagle and his nails like the claws of a bird. At the end of that time, I, Nebuchadnezzar, raised my eyes toward heaven, and my sanity was restored. Then I praised the Most High; I honored and glorified him who lives forever. His dominion is an eternal dominion; his kingdom endures from generation to generation." (Daniel 4:28-34)*

Sometimes our distress comes even after God warns us through our dreams and through other people. The king was not repentant right away. It took seven years for him to realize that his loss was caused by his pride. After he repented, God restored what the king had lost.

We need to look in our hearts and see if we have distress or trouble caused by a proud attitude instead of giving God glory, honor, and praise for what God has done in our lives. If we do, we need to repent.

Prayer: "Lord, All the good things I have in life come from you. If I have distress and pain because of my sin, please help me to learn and not fall into the sin of pride. Fill my heart with joy and peace. Deliver me from pain and anguish. If there is any other thing that I need to change, please show it to me so I can repent and make changes."

6. Jesus – Sorrowful and troubled to the point of death

Jesus didn't commit any sin or anything to deserve death. But, He faced torture, humiliation, pain, suffering and death on the cross for our sins. Matthew describes how Jesus endured the pain and anguish.

"Then Jesus went with his disciples to a place called Gethsemane, and he said to them, 'Sit here while I go over there and pray.' he took Peter and the two sons of Zebedee along with him, and he began to be sorrowful and troubled. Then he said to them, 'My soul is overwhelmed with sorrow to the point of death. Stay here and keep watch with me.' Going a little farther, he fell with his face to the ground and prayed, 'My Father, if it is possible, may this cup be taken from me. Yet not as I will, but as you will.'" (Matthew 26:36-39)

Jesus not only understands our pain and suffering because He had gone through it, but He also teaches us how to handle difficult times. There are times we don't have any control of what is going to happen in our lives, like losing our health, losing jobs, losing material things that we value and/or losing our loved ones. When that happens, we can be immobilized with grief and pain.

We need to rely on God for intervention, healing, understanding, and wisdom to deal with our grief and loss. God can help us find peace in our heart if only we follow Jesus' example: 1) Pray, pray, and pray. Pray to God for intervention, peace, guidance, understanding, and the wisdom to share how you feel when you are in trouble; 2) Give everything to God because there are things that are not in our control. Everything we have is a temporary gift; 3) Seeking God's will, not ours, to be done in our lives.

Prayer: "Lord Jesus, thank you for your suffering and death on the cross for my sins. You understand my pain and suffering. Help me to understand your will for my life and help me rely on you for everything. I give you all my grief, grievance and pain. Help me find peace and joy in you."

7. Paul — Felt the sentence of death

After Paul started preaching, he was persecuted and suffered greatly. Still, he wouldn't give up and he teaches us how to handle difficult times.

He states, *"Praise be to the God and Father of our Lord Jesus Christ, the Father of compassion and the God of all comfort, who comforts us in all our troubles, so that we can comfort those in any trouble with the comfort we ourselves have received from God. For just as the sufferings of Christ flow over into our lives, so also through Christ our comfort overflows. If we are distressed, it is for your comfort and salvation; if we are comforted, it is for your comfort, which produces in you patient endurance of the same sufferings we suffer. And our hope for you is firm, because we know that just as you share in our sufferings, so also you share in our comfort. We do not want you to be uninformed, brothers, about the hardships we suffered in the province of Asia. We were under great pressure, far beyond our ability to endure, so that we despaired even of life. Indeed, in our hearts we felt the sentence of death. But this happened that we might not rely on ourselves but on God, who raises the dead." (2 Corinthians 1:3-9)*

Paul didn't do anything wrong. He was suffering because he was serving God. If you are doing something good and are misunderstood or persecuted, ask the Lord to protect you.

Prayer: "Jesus, I ask you to deliver me from all false accusations. Please help me to have complete trust in you and help me to focus on loving you and serving you. Bless me with wisdom, knowledge, understanding and revelation on how to deal with my problems your way."

Chapter 7

Spiritual Prescription for the Depressed Mind

1. Process Your Pains One by One

When you feel overwhelmed, find out which area you need to work on. The following exercises can help you clear your mind and help you find peace and healing.

Reflect: Try to understand what you are suffering from, like unforgiveness, anger, bitterness, hated, or grief from a loss, a spirit of despair etc.

Repent: Repenting is the first process in your healing. One by one, ask the Lord to forgive you if you have sinned against God or someone else. If you are suffering from spiritual oppression, there is a reason and you somehow have opened the door to the spirits. By repenting, you are asking God to help you and cleanse you. You will be strengthened in this spiritual battle if you have a clean heart. That clean heart is the result of repenting of your sins.

Repenting is humbling yourself. *"Come near to God and he will come near to you. Wash your hands, you sinners, and purify your hearts, you double-minded. Grieve, mourn and wail. Change your laughter to mourning and your joy to gloom. Humble yourselves before the Lord, and he will lift you up."* (James 4:8-10) *"For surely, O Lord, you bless the righteous; you surround them with your favor as with a shield."* (Psalm 5:12)

If you are forgiven by God and try to walk with Jesus, you can have confidence like Paul. He wrote, *"What, then, shall we say in response to this? If God is for us, who can be against us? He who did not spare his own Son, but gave him up for us all--how will he not also, along with him, graciously give us all things? Who will bring any charge against those whom God has chosen? It is God who justifies. Who is he that condemns? Christ Jesus, who died--more than that, who was raised to life--is at the right hand of God and is also interceding for us. Who shall separate us from the love of Christ? Shall trouble or hardship or persecution or famine or nakedness or danger or sword?" (Romans 8:31-35)*

Those who are grieving also need to take care of the painful emotions related to your loss. Then, you need to let your loved ones go in order to be healed from sadness, pain and triggers caused by your loss.

Prayer: "Lord Jesus, please help me in my grieving process so I can experience healing. I give my loved ones to you. Please take away any desire to be with my loved ones. Help me focus on loving you and take caring of others who are in need of my love and attention."

Search: Find Scriptures that will give you direction on how to handle your struggles according to God's Word. The Word of God will give you the wisdom to handle things so you don't have to be in pain or confused.

Process: Process your pain and take care of your problems and issues through prayer and confession. Ask God for the wisdom to understand others and your situations. The more you take care of the areas of hurts and pain, the more you will find peace and not be overwhelmed.

Pray: When the disciples were faced with storms, they asked Jesus to help them. Jesus rebuked the sea and told them to have faith. *"He said to his disciples, 'Why are you so afraid? Do you still have no faith?' They were terrified and asked each other, 'Who is this? Even the wind and the waves obey him!'" (Mark 4:40-41)*

Focus: Be proactive taking care of yourself so you don't fall into depression. Focus on positive things and blessings you have received from the Lord.

John wrote, *"From the fullness of his grace we have all received one blessing after another." (John 1:16)* The more we learn to see what God is doing in our lives to bless us even in hard times, we can become stronger. The Word of God says, *"When you pass through the waters, I will be with you; and when you pass through the rivers, they will not sweep over you. When you walk through the fire, you will not be burned; the flames will not set you ablaze." (Isaiah 43:2)*

Find: You are not alone in this battle. Many others have walked the same path have experienced pain and came out of depression. They can help you find a way out. If you don't have a spiritual mentor who can help you, ask the Lord to help you find a godly, spiritual mentor. Someone who can guide you to live a righteous life and pray for you. Have positive people around you and that will help you see the big picture.

Repeat: If you still suffer from negative emotions that overwhelm you, follow the same pattern and continue the process until you can let it go.

The following are some examples of how you can learn to process different areas that trouble you.

(1) Anger and an Unforgiving Heart

Many depressed people suffer from anger, resentment, and bitterness. We need to learn to rely on God for understanding and wisdom to deal with people and situations so we don't keep piling up problems. Go to "Spiritual Prescription 5. Forgive everyone." Reflect, meditate, and follow the spiritual practices. Pray for wisdom so you will learn to forgive.

Prayer: "Lord, help me to have your wisdom and insight to understand myself and others so I can forgive."

(2) Grief and Loss

Many who suffer from depression have suffered grief and loss. When they are healed from grief and pain, they will no longer suffer from depression. You need to realize that everything we have is temporary.

Learn to appreciate what you have and not continuously grieve for the loss. Read Job and find out how he dealt with loss. Grieving brings many more issues. When you grieve you are in a grieving room and need to visit many rooms and take care of it before you get out.

See which areas you need to work on: anger, resentment, bitterness, regrets, forgiveness, attachment, letting go, repentance and other emotions. People who don't know how to process emotions caused by grief and loss can be immobilized with pain and cannot move on.

If you are suffering from grief and loss, I ask you to go over all the areas and start writing it down and ask the Lord for healing. Write letters to process healing like: forgiveness letters, love letters, goodbye letters, etc.

Prayer: "Lord Jesus, please help me in my grief and pain. I need you to heal my broken heart. Please help me to let go of all my pain and my loved ones so I can go on with my life. I rely on you for healing. Help me to have your wisdom and understanding. Take away all the desires and hurts that are related to the loss of my loved one. I depend on you for healing. I forgive everyone including myself. Help me to be healed from pain caused by my loss and grief. Help me to be released from any kind of triggers and memories that are making my heart sad and depressed. I am looking up to you and I rely on you for healing of my broken heart. Please release me from this spiritual prison of grief and sadness. I rejoice in you, Lord, because all I have are temporary gifts but you have given me the permanent gift of my relationship with you. Lord Jesus, you are my joy and strength. I believe in you. Fill my heart with hope and joy so I can help others who are grieving and hurting. I pray this in Jesus' name."

(3) Abused and Traumatized

Many people who have been abused or have been in a scary and horrifying situation suffer from depression. They are haunted by their past and overwhelmed with fear and cannot move on.

If you are suffering from traumatic experiences, I encourage you to write them down and ask the Lord for healing of your mind and heart. God can heal your memories and restore you so you can function normally. If you are struggling with triggers, that means you need healing. I have seen many who suffered from Post Traumatic Stress Disorder healed with God's healing power. Let's ask the Lord for healing and not give up on hope that you will be able to function normally and move forward positively in life.

Prayer: "Lord Jesus, I have experienced so much trauma, and I struggle with triggers. My spirit has been broken and shattered. Heal my memories so I don't have to suffer from my painful memories. I put myself in your big hands. I am asking you to touch and heal me. Give me a new heart that is filled with strength, wisdom, hope, joy and peace. Bless me with faith so that I will be able to rely on you for healing of mind and heart. I forgive everyone who has hurt me. I let go of all my anger, resentment and bitterness toward anyone and any situation. Knowing that you can help me heal from my past, give me a new heart with hope and direction on how I can help others who are hurting. Give me clear direction on how to help others who are hurting. I am looking into the future that I can be your heart and hands to help others. Thank you Lord Jesus for healing me and giving me a new heart. I pray this in Jesus' name. Amen."

(4) Self-hate or Self-mutilation

Some people who suffer from depression don't know how to love and respect themselves. They suffer from self-hate and hurt themselves by cutting themselves, saying that their pain is so great and hurting themselves relieves pain. How can a person say that physical pain will relieve emotional pain? There is a way to relieve emotional pain and that is through God by first repenting that you have not taken care of your body which God has given you to take care of and not to abuse.

If you are cutting your body because you are in so much pain, Jesus can heal you. He healed a man who was cutting himself and tormented. Don't accept suggestions to hurt yourself in anyway. Don't accept the lies of the devil because it will cause you more pain.

God wants you to love and take care of your soul and body because He loves you and bought you. He paid the price by dying on the cross. He offers us forgiveness and freed us from the spiritual prison of torment. You should immediately turn to the Lord for help if you hear a voice telling you to hurt yourself.

Prayer: "Lord Jesus, I am in so much pain and I need you to heal me from the spirit of torment. Please forgive me for the sins of hurting myself. I have not taken care of your property which is my body as you would want me to. I ask you to help me so I can stop hurting my body that was created for you and by you. Lord Jesus, you died on the cross for my sins. I ask you to help free me from this torment and pain. Come Holy Spirit, come and free me from this torment. Fill my heart with your love and power to overcome the lies of the devil that, cutting myself is a way to ease my pain. I forgive everyone who has hurt me. I forgive myself for not following your ways. I ask you to forgive me for any sins that I have committed. Wash me with the blood of Jesus and cleanse me from all my sins. I ask for your mercy and compassion. If there is any sin I haven't repented or if I need to change my attitudes and actions, please let me know. Lord Jesus, come into my heart and fill it with your love. I believe you died on the cross to save me and shed your blood for my sins. Free me from this prison of self-hate and anger. I ask you to give me a new heart that is filled with love and compassion for myself and others. Help me to understand the purpose of my life so I can serve you the way you want me to serve you. I thank you and praise you, Lord Jesus, for helping me. Help me to understand what kind of changes I need to make in my everyday life so I don't fall into the trap of spiritual prison and self-hate. Please help me. Come now, Lord Jesus, for your sake and save me from the tormenting demons so I can find peace and joy in you. I am not going to believe the lies that lead me to cut myself and to forget my emotional pain. Help me to love you and serve you. Help me, Holy Spirit, I need your peace and joy. I pray this in Jesus' name."

(5) Despair and Suicidal Thoughts

Some people hear voices that life is not worthwhile and no one cares about them. They hear voices that they are useless and that they are a burden to others. When they accept these voices, they open the door for the spirits of torment. The spirit of torment literally torments people with much pain. These people hear voices that their pain will end when they end their lives. If they continuously accept the lies and do not resist the voices, they can be suicidal and can commit suicide.

Life is a gift from the Lord. Don't let the devil lie to you that pain is what life is about. Yes, life is difficult and painful at times, but God can bring healing. The spirit of despair tries to undermine the power of God which can help us heal from pain and hurts and gives us peace and joy in the midst of turmoil.

You need to rely on the Word of God, not your own understanding. God values us. Jesus came and died for our sins. He opened the door for salvation and to allow us to build a relationship with God. God values us so we should value ourselves.

Prayer: "Lord Jesus, I am in pain and I ask you to help me get out of this mess. Help me to find healing in you. I ask for your forgiveness for all my sins including devaluing my life and what you have given me. Please forgive all my sins and help me change my perception so I can see myself as you see me. Help me to understand your Words so I can have clear direction on how to love and serve you. Help me to understand your love and help me to love myself. Help me to reach out to others who are hurting with your love and power."

(6) Addiction, Guilt or Shame

If you are constantly bombarded with guilt and shame, there is something that you need to change. If you keep falling into addictive lifestyles like alcohol, drugs, sexual sin, anger, worries, fear, an unforgiving heart, and other sins that you know are hurting you, your family, or others, you need to repent and ask God for forgiveness and change your lifestyle. Repenting is what some people need to do to experience healing from a depressed mind. Don't allow any room for the devil to accuse you. The devil also wants you to accuse yourself so you cannot focusing on the Lord, but focusing on hurting yourself and condemning yourself. Repentance is the cleansing of our hearts. It frees us from accusations from the devil and brings us peace and joy.

Write a confession letter going back to your childhood as far as you can remember. Write your sins down and ask God to forgive you, one by one. Also, if you haven't forgiven yourself or others, ask God to help you. Let go of the blame and bitterness. If you love people or things more than God, you need to repent and change your priorities. As long as you love people and things more than God, you are inviting turmoil because we are created to love God. That's not a recommendation but a command from the Lord.

Prayer: "Lord Jesus, please forgive my destructive behaviors of loving the world more than you. I have hurt myself and others with an addictive lifestyle of sin and destruction. Please forgive me. I need you to help me to recognize what I love more than you so I can learn to love you more than anyone or anything, such as my addictive, impure thoughts or addictions. Please forgive me for all the things I put into my body to hurt myself and for neglecting my family's needs. Help me to recognize impure desires, thoughts, attitudes, words and actions that displease you and hurt others. I made a decision to change my life and work on loving you more than anyone or anything. Help me to repent from all my sins. Holy Spirit, remind me if there is sin that I need to repent. Lord Jesus, bless me with a clear conscience so I can see things as you see them. Bless me with faith that gives me the determination to make changes so I can love you. Forgive me for holding anger, resentment and an unforgiving heart toward people who hurt me. I forgive everyone, including myself. Please help me to repent if there is any sin that is displeasing you. Help me to change. I also forgive myself and others who have hurt me. I have decided to love you and serve you. Let me hear from you, if there is anything that I need to do to please you. Help me to focus on you and take away any desire for an addictive lifestyle so I can live a pure, holy, and blameless life that will bring healing. Help me to help others who are in need of your healing. Amen."

(7) Worry and Fear

Many who are depressed have been hurt, but they never process their worries or fears so their perception can be clouded. Some suffer from their worries and fears to the point that they are consumed with what could happen to them or their loved ones. The spirit of worry and fear plague many people.

Some who are depressed isolate themselves because that makes them feel safe. Their activities and relationships are neglected by worry and fear. The Scripture teaches us not to worry; it's time to read the Bible more and repent of our lack of belief in the Lord to take care of us.

Jesus said, *"Come to me, all you who are weary and burdened, and I will give you rest. Take my yoke upon you and learn from me, for I am gentle and humble in heart, and you will find rest for your souls. For my yoke is easy and my burden is light." (Matthew 11:28-30)*

Prayer: "Lord Jesus, I look to you for healing of my wearied and fearful heart. Help me to do the things that I need to do to find peace and joy. Help me to have faith in you so I can live by faith, not by fear. Help me to rely on you and not my own strength or wisdom. I give you all my worries and fear because you can help me and free me from the spirit of worry and fear. I give you myself, my loved ones, my finances and everything that concerns me. Help me take care of what you have given me with your wisdom and strength. I rely on your love and grace. I proclaim victory in Jesus that I will not meditate on problems but will look to you for wisdom and help to solve problems. I am waiting on you, Lord. Please speak to me so I can understand what I need to find peace and joy. Lord Jesus, you are my joy and peace. Help me so I look to you for answers for my problems. Please speak to me."

Spiritual Prescription

2. Love God

We are created by God to love and worship Him. Loving God has to be our highest priority and loving other people has to be second. Many of our problems arise because we love people and things more than God. Check and see if you love anything or anyone more than the Lord. If you do, it's time to change your priorities.

"Love the Lord your God with all your heart and with all your soul and with all your mind and with all your strength. The second is this: 'Love your neighbor as yourself.' There is no commandment greater than these." (Mark 12:30-31)

Prayer: "Lord Jesus, I love you. Please forgive me for loving things and people more than you. Please cleanse me from all my sin and fill my heart with love for you so that my love will grow daily, moment by moment. Help me so I don't become distracted by people or things of this world. Thank you for your gifts of people and things that I need. I realize that they are temporary gifts from you, and I ask you to help remind me that you are the one I need in order to experience complete healing from my depression. Fill me with the Holy Spirit and give me direction on how to love you more. I pray this in Jesus' name. Amen."

How to focus on loving God:

Paul tells us that Jesus is God and created us and we are created for him. He wrote, *"giving thanks to the Father, who has qualified you to share in the inheritance of the saints in the kingdom of light. For he has rescued us from the dominion of darkness and brought us into the kingdom of the Son he loves, in whom we have redemption, the forgiveness of sins. He is the image of the invisible God, the firstborn over all creation. For by him all things were created: things in heaven and on earth, visible and invisible, whether thrones or powers or rulers or authorities; all things were created by him and for him. He is before all things, and in him all things hold together." (Colossians 1:12-17)* Jesus is God and loving Him is loving God. To love someone, you need to know the person.

Get to know Jesus: Your relationship with the Lord Jesus is very important in your healing process because He has the power to heal your hurts and pain. You will be gaining spiritual power when you rely on Jesus to help you because he cares for you and died on the cross for your sins. Read the gospel (Matthew, Mark, Luke or John) 30 minutes a day or read one gospel a day out loud for the next 30 days. *"And without faith it is impossible to please God, because anyone who comes to him must believe that he exists and that he rewards those who earnestly seek him." (Hebrews 11:6)*

Worship Jesus: Find ways throughout the day to worship, praise, and thank Him. Tell Jesus you love Him whenever you think about him. This is a good start as you remind yourself that you are created for the Lord, to love the Lord. As you get to know Jesus through the Word and express your love for the Lord, your love for the Lord will grow. Attend church worship services, Bible studies, and prayer meetings to help focus on him and love him. Read the Bible and learn about how others love the Lord.

Prayer: "Lord, I give you all my worries, fears, and anything that is hindering my love for you. Give me a new heart that is filled with love for you."

Praise Jesus: Always praise the Lord, especially in times of trouble. Praising Jesus is good medicine for our troubled soul and sorrowful times. Our pain will start healing when we seek God and start praising Him for what He can do to help us. Praising God pleases Him. He can help us see how much power He has over everything. We can learn to see the big picture and God's plans for us. Sing a song for Jesus every day.

Bless the Lord: God said to Abraham, *"I will make you into a great nation and I will bless you; I will make your name great, and you will be a blessing. I will bless those who bless you, and whoever curses you I will curse; and all peoples on earth will be blessed through you." (Genesis 12:2-3)* This Scripture tells me how much God wants to bless us and we should do the same.

Prayer: "Lord Jesus, I will announce to the world how great you are and I will bless you. I will announce to the world that you are a great God and I will bless those who love you. I pray that all the earth will be blessed through your great love for us through Jesus Christ who died for our sins."

Focus on Jesus and don't be afraid of life's storms: Many people who suffer from depression focus on their problems more than God. Their pain will grow if they only focus on pain. They try to understand their problems on their own, and they can't find peace or healing.

Our own understanding and wisdom have limits and we need to be active in guiding our thoughts. Being sad or having depressed thoughts cannot guide us. Many people have problems because they are not active managing their thoughts. They let the enemy plant seeds of doubt, fear, worry and negative thoughts which will lead to depression.

Prayer: "Lord Jesus, help me to love you with all my heart, soul, mind and strength."

Write a love letter: 1) Write a love letter to Jesus; 2) Write a love letter from Jesus to you; 3) Write a forgiveness letter from God; 4) Write a letter to God asking for forgiveness; 5) Write a victory prayer to be healed from depression.

Obey the Word of God: Another important part of loving Jesus is obeying the Lord. Jesus tells us to love one another and obey the Lord. *"Whoever has my commands and obeys them, he is the one who loves me. He who loves me will be loved by my Father, and I too will love him and show myself to him." (John 14:21) "If anyone loves me, he will obey my teaching. My Father will love him, and we will come to him and make our home with him. He who does not love me will not obey my teaching. These words you hear are not my own; they belong to the Father who sent me." (John 14:23-24) "The goal of this command is love, which comes from a pure heart and a good conscience and a sincere faith." (1 Timothy 1:5)*

You can invite Jesus: How can you love God if you have not accepted Jesus as your Lord and Savior? If you don't have a relationship with Jesus, this is your opportunity to invite Him into your life.

Prayer: "Lord Jesus, I give my life to you. I open my heart and invite you into my life. I am a sinner. Please forgive me and baptize me with the Holy Spirit. Please help me to understand your love. Bless me with a new heart so I will love you and willingly serve you. I pray this in Jesus' name. Amen."

Spiritual Prescription

3. Love Yourself

To experience healing from a depressed mind, we need to be freed from self-condemnation and learn to see ourselves as God sees us - beloved and precious in His sight.

"For God so loved the world that he gave his one and only Son, that whoever believes in him shall not perish but have eternal life." (John 3:16) "We love because he first loved us." (1 John 4:19)

Many people who suffer from depression have a difficult time loving themselves because they value themselves according to how they have been treated by others. So, many people suffer from the spirit of despair, hatred, inferiority and lack of self-esteem. People create a value system according to their culture and society values. Most of their values are not affirming but devaluing certain people and it affects us negatively. Many people hear voices saying that nothing, including life or themselves, are worthy because of how they have been treated.

When God created you, He was pleased with you. He values you and He wants you to be happy. Jesus came and died for our sins so we can have a close relationship with Him. If you devalue yourself and others, it's time to shake off the negative thoughts that are plaguing you and eating you up. Start mediating on the Scriptures that helps you value yourself and others. You need to develop a habit of loving yourself.

I was once talking to a person who was always smiling. She shared with me that everyday she looks in the mirror and says, "I love you and you are special." I think it's great she recognizes her value. She needs to love herself.

I encourage you to do that if you need to remind yourself that you love yourself or whenever you feel bad about yourself or make a mistake.

Also, you can tell yourself:

- I am beautifully and wonderfully made and created by God.
- I am special because I am loved by God.
- I am created for the divine purpose of giving God glory.
- I am a reflection of God's glory.
- I am valuable to God and His kingdom business.
- God created me in His image.
- I am precious in God's sight.
- I am created to be a partner in God's kingdom building business.
- I am a conqueror of the dark world and the devil cannot stand against me.
- I am a child of God because I believe in Jesus.
- I am clothed with Christ so the Holy Spirit is working with me.
- I am blessed beyond measure, and I will be a blessing to others.
- God didn't make a mistake creating me.
- God has visions, dreams, and plans for my life.
- I am worthy of God's love because Jesus died for my sins.
- I am filled with the Holy Spirit who can bring healing.
- I am forgiven. God has forgotten my mistakes and failures.
- I am hopeful because I know Jesus is preparing a place for me.
- I am encouraged that my trials and difficulties are a

purifying fire.

- I am joyful because the Holy Spirit is leading my path.
- I value myself and others because God values us.
- I am hopeful because God is going to help me overcome depression.
- I am blessed that God is training me to be a disciple of Jesus.

Prayer: "Lord Jesus, help me to understand your love so I can learn to love myself and others. Help me to value myself and others so I can love you, love myself and love others as well. Thank you Lord Jesus for loving me and dying on the cross to forgive me. Please fill my heart with love for you, myself and others. Help me to love as you love me. Please forgive me for not loving myself. Cleanse me from all my guilt and shame. Free me from the unforgiving spirits and fill my heart with loving spirits. Help me to love what you have given me – my life, all my family and other people you created in your image."

"But the fruit of the spirit is love, joy, peace, patience, kindness, goodness, faithfulness, gentleness and self-control. Against such things there is no law. Those who belong to Christ Jesus have crucified the sinful nature with its passions and desires. Since we live by the Spirit, let us keep in step with the Spirit. Let us not become conceited, provoking and envying each other." (Galatians 5:22-26)

Spiritual Prescription

4. Meditate on the Word of God

Many who are depressed have no passion for life, themselves or others. With God's help, we can find passion and love for the Lord, ourselves, and others. This can happen when you spend time reading the Bible and start meditating on it. Don't just read it, but learn to recognize confusing thoughts and get rid of them. Then you will find the peace God gives you.

One reason we can be depressed is because we try to understand our life through our own wisdom and understanding. The more you store the Word of God in your thought bank, the more you will be able to experience healing from depression.

"My son, pay attention to what I say; listen closely to my words. Do not let them out of your sight, keep them within your heart; for they are life to those who find them and health to a man's whole body. Above all else, guard your heart, for it is the wellspring of life. Put away perversity from your mouth; keep corrupt talk far from your lips. Let your eyes look straight ahead, fix your gaze directly before you. Make level paths for your feet and take only ways that are firm. Do not swerve to the right or the left; keep your foot from evil." (Proverbs 4:20-27)

Our lack of knowledge of the Scriptures is one of the reasons why we cannot hear the voice of God. God can speak to us in many ways but He mostly speaks to us through the Word of God. Learning to listen to God's instructions through the Word of God has to be the most important process in our healing journey.

Even if you have been reading the Bible, if you have been affected by too many hurtful voices, the devil will influence your way of thinking when you read the Bible.

If you are so filled with confusing voices when you try to read the Bible, you may try to twist the Word of God to fit your own sinful thoughts and behaviors. That's one of the reasons why some people interpret the Bible to permit them to commit sin. We need to watch how we interpret the Bible. We need God's help on this.

Prayer: "Holy Spirit, bless me with spiritual wisdom, knowledge, understanding and revelation so I can understand the Bible as you want me to. Surround me with Your angels and protect me from twisted thinking."

You need to know that the more you accept destructive voices, the more you will suffer from hopelessness, helplessness, sadness, and feelings of despair. It's crucial to start reading the Bible so you can understand God's truth and resist the voices that confuse you.

Be aware of how you spend your time everyday and every moment so you can transform your thoughts and behaviors. This practice is not passive thinking where the enemy can attack, but we are taking over our thoughts with God's Word to chase the thoughts that are dark and confusing. As you apply God's Word to different areas and are active in your healing process, your foggy mind will start to clear little by little.

If you plant worldly, flesh, and sinful seeds in your hearts you will see the poisonous fruits of depression. You will see good fruit when you plant the seeds of peace, joy, encouragement, and comfort.

Here are questions that you can ask yourself for your self-assessment of how you spend your time each day and what you put in your thought bank:

(1) How much time do you spend focusing on your problems? (24 hours, even in your dreams? Or just

when you are awake? About 1 hour?)

(2) Do you try to solve your problems through your own understanding? (Most of the time or all the time?)

(3) Do you rely on other's advice for solving problems? (A little, most of the time or all the time)

(4) How much time do you spend watching TV or reading books that help your spiritual growth? (30 minutes, 2 hours, or all the time)

(5) How much time do you spend reading the Bible, meditating and praying? (30 minutes, 2 hours, or all the time)

How did you do? Did you see where you are? How you spend your time will determine if you can be delivered from confused or depressed thoughts. Many people do not realize why they are sad and depressed. You can only produce what you have planted. How much time you spend with your thoughts and effort focused on God, praying and reading the Word of God will determine how fast you will be able to process your twisted thinking to life -giving, clear thoughts. In order to do that, you need to develop a new nature and habit.

Start reading the Bible, meditating on it, and speaking the Word to your mind. Start speaking the Word and start acting on it.

Find Bible verses to fight the negative voices in your mind to overcome depression. God's Word gives us power to overcome negative, critical, and destructive voices. Healing will come when we learn to rely on God and apply God's Word in the areas in which we struggle. Meditate on the Word of God day and night, that's what God told Joshua to do. *(Joshua 1:1-9)*

Develop a 30-day Bible reading: Make a habit of relying on God and His Word for continued healing from emotional and spiritual pain. You can start reading the gospels (Matthew, Mark, Luke, and John) to get to know Jesus or read Proverbs one chapter a day to gain God's wisdom and spiritual understanding. Find any part of Scripture that touches you and keep reading it, even though you may not understand it. Ask the Lord for wisdom to understand it. Meditate on or read any part of the Bible that gives you comfort. Read continuously and God will give you wisdom and understanding.

Read Psalms and find prayers that help you express your feelings. Ask God for help. Try to find a Bible verse that touches you, meditate and memorize it throughout the day. *"Trust in the Lord with all your heart and lean not on your own understanding; in all your ways acknowledge him, and he will make your paths straight. Do not be wise in your own eyes; fear the Lord and shun evil. This will bring health to your body and nourishment to your bones." (Proverbs 3:5-8)*

Attend worship services, Bible study, prayer meetings, and find a mature spiritual mentor who can help you understand the Bible and how to apply what you read. Read Christian books that will help you understand your spiritual journey.

Resist twisted Interpretation: Many people who suffer from depression have a hard time reading the Bible because the devil twists the meaning of the Word of God. The devil does that to discourage people from reading the Bible. When you hear voices that make you confused, don't stop reading the Bible. Rebuke the devil by saying, "In the name of Jesus I rebuke you, the devil of lies, to leave me."

Memorize Luke 4:18-19: *"The Spirit of the Lord is on me, because he has anointed me to preach good news to the poor. He has sent me to proclaim freedom for the prisoners and recovery of sight for the blind, to release the oppressed, to proclaim the year of the Lord's favor." (Luke 4:18-19)*

This Scripture is talking about what Jesus can do for

each of us who believe in God. We have the Holy Spirit's anointing to help ourselves free from a spiritual prison. Unless we are freed, we cannot help others. Keep meditating on the Word of God to learn about God. Understand who you are in Christ and what God wants you to do with your life.

Prayer: "Lord Jesus come, Holy Spirit come, Father God come and bless me with wisdom and understanding of the Bible. Holy Spirit, I ask you to surround me with warrior angels and protect me from the devil's attacks and lies so that I will be able to understand the correct meaning of the Bible. Lord Jesus, anoint me with the Holy Spirit and protect me from distraction so I can focus on you, Lord. I pray this in the name of Jesus. Amen."

Spiritual Prescription

5. Forgive Everyone

"Finally, all of you, live in harmony with one another; be sympathetic, love as brothers, be compassionate and humble. Do not repay evil with evil or insult with insult, but with blessing, because to this you were called so that you may inherit a blessing. For, 'Whoever would love life and see good days must keep his tongue from evil and his lips from deceitful speech. He must turn from evil and do good; he must seek peace and pursue it. For the eyes of the Lord are on the righteous and his ears are attentive to their prayer, but the face of the Lord is against those who do evil.'" (1 Peter 3:9-12) "Above all, love each other deeply, because love covers over a multitude of sins." (1 Peter 4:8)

Many people who are depressed suffer from anger, resentment, bitterness and an unforgiving spirit. Forgive everyone, including yourself. If you don't forgive, you are opening the door to the devil and spiritual attacks which can immobilize you with pain, hindering you from gaining peace. You will be in a spiritual prison of torment.

Write a confession letter: If you want to forgive but you cannot, write a confession letter asking God to forgive you for holding onto the spirit of unforgiveness. Don't look at others, but look at yourself first and see what God is telling you about the situation. Jesus tells us the spiritual prescription for forgiveness: forgive, pray and bless them.

Misconception of forgiveness: Some people think they need to accept abuse and stay in abusive or violent situations because the Bible says that you should forgive. Forgiveness doesn't mean you give others permission to abuse you. You need to forgive others, but not to the point that you put yourself in a dangerous situation where you feel helpless, hopeless, anger, rage and hatred.

There are some abusive situations and relationships that you need to be freed from before you can forgive. Don't beat yourself down, but try to solve the problems according to God's wisdom. Ask others to help you if you cannot figure out what to do. After you are removed from abusive situations and problems are resolved, if you are still suffering from an unforgiving spirit, you need to ask for forgiveness from God. Forgive yourself and others by letting go of that person or situation.

You need to find peace with God, yourself and others with God's wisdom. Sometimes you have to break from a relationship to get away from "porcupine" people to find peace so you can forgive. Sometimes you might have to find a different job to find peace.

Write forgiveness letters: Write a forgiveness letter to everyone to whom you feel angry and resentful. You don't have to send it out, only if it will be helpful to everyone. Write a letter of forgiveness to yourself if you suffer from guilt and shame.

Bless and pray for others: The devil will try to keep reminding you about painful experiences to make you bitter and angry. Pray and bless others every time those memories come up. Then, gradually and eventually the unforgiving spirit will leave and you will find peace and healing. Healing is a process.

"But I tell you who hear me: Love your enemies, do good to those who hate you, bless those who curse you, pray for those who mistreat you." (Luke 6:27-28) "You have heard that it was said, 'Love your neighbor and hate your enemy.' But I tell you: Love your enemies and pray for those who persecute you." (Matthew 5:43-44)

"Bless those who persecute you; bless and do not curse. Rejoice with those who rejoice; mourn with those who mourn. Live in harmony with one another. Do not be proud, but be

willing to associate with people of low position. Do not be conceited. Do not repay anyone evil for evil. Be careful to do what is right in the eyes of everybody. If it is possible, as far as it depends on you, live at peace with everyone. Do not take revenge, my friends, but leave room for God's wrath, for it is written: 'It is mine to avenge; I will repay,' says the Lord. On the contrary: 'If your enemy is hungry, feed him; if he is thirsty, give him something to drink. In doing this, you will heap burning coals on his head.' Do not be overcome by evil, but overcome evil with good." (Romans 12:14-21) "If we confess our sins, he is faithful and just and will forgive us our sins and purify us from all unrighteousness." (1 John 1:9-10)

We have no right to hold on to an unforgiving spirit for ourselves or others because Jesus died for us. *"Whoever does not love does not know God, because God is love. This is how God showed his love among us: He sent his one and only Son into the world that we might live through him. This is love: not that we loved God, but that he loved us and sent his Son as an atoning sacrifice for our sins. Dear friends, since God so loved us, we also ought to love one another. No one has ever seen God; but if we love one another, God lives in us and his love is made complete in us. We know that we live in him and he in us, because he has given us of his Spirit." (1 John 4:8-13)*

Prayer: "God, release me from my destructive, negative, and critical thoughts and attitudes. Help me develop a loving attitude, even toward those who have hurt me. Forgive my unforgiving spirit. I ask you to transform me by replacing it with a forgiving spirit. If there is sin I have not repented, help me repent. Please speak to me, Lord Jesus, I am waiting. Lord Jesus, help me understand your great love. Please forgive all my sins. Cleanse me with the blood of Jesus. You died for my sins. This I believe, so free me now from the guilt and shame I feel. Lord Jesus, it is my desire to forgive everyone who has hurt me. Fill me with your Spirit of love and compassion.

Bless everyone, including those who have hurt me. Please restore in my heart a spirit of love and respect toward everyone."

Change your perception of others:

See the big picture. There is no one who is completely good or bad. Everyone has good in them, even those who have hurt us, because we are all created in the image of God. I believe everyone has 85% of the godly character that God has given us. We all have the capacity to do good as long as we resist sinful desires and follow our God-given character.

Paul wrote, *"Therefore, I urge you, brothers, in view of God's mercy, to offer your bodies as living sacrifices, holy and pleasing to God--this is your spiritual act of worship. Do not conform any longer to the pattern of this world, but be transformed by the renewing of your mind. Then you will be able to test and approve what God's will is--his good, pleasing and perfect will." (Romans 12:1-2)*

We also have 15% of the dark side which are sinful desires, unforgiving spirits, and bad character traits. This dark side needs to be transformed in order for us to learn how to forgive. The devil encourages us to fall into sin by appealing to our dark side. With no knowledge of God's Word, we are victims of our own ignorance.

We can follow the Holy Spirit's lead and the 85% of goodness, our God-given character, will come forth. If you don't have a relationship with Jesus, invite him into your heart and ask him to help you so you can learn to forgive and find peace. People who cannot forgive cannot have peace. People who have not been forgiven by God do not have peace.

Prayer: "Lord Jesus, I give my life to you. Please come into my heart, my life and forgive my sins. I believe you died on the cross for my sins and I am saved because of what you have done for me. Fill me with your Holy Spirit and teach me to forgive myself and others so I can find peace. Amen."

Spiritual Prescription

6. Resist Twisted Logic

If you have accepted destructive thoughts or voices from the spirit of despair, you may suffer from hopelessness, helplessness, sadness, despair, a foggy mind, and spiritual oppression. The Holy Spirit's conviction of sins will bring repentance, forgiveness and healing in our hearts and mind. Thus, we find peace and joy in God. If your thoughts are not leading you to peace but to turmoil, be aware that you may be suffering from hurtful thoughts and voices.

The Lord has the power to help you because He has blessed you with the Holy Spirit. *"You, dear children, are from God and have overcome them, because the one who is in you is greater than the one who is in the world." (1 John 4:4)*

Peter teaches us how to resist the devil. *"Cast all your anxiety on him because he cares for you. Be self-controlled and alert. Your enemy the devil prowls around like a roaring lion looking for someone to devour. Resist him, standing firm in the faith, because you know that your brothers throughout the world are undergoing the same kind of sufferings." (1 Peter 5:7-9)*

You need to learn to fight the hurtful voices with the Word of God. Healing is a process so don't give up when you don't see progress right away. Keep reading His Word and pray and ask the Lord to give you wisdom and strength.

"Who is wise and understanding among you? Let him show it by his good life, by deeds done in the humility that comes from wisdom. But if you harbor bitter envy and selfish ambition in your hearts, do not boast about it or deny the truth. Such 'wisdom' does not come down from heaven but is earthly,

unspiritual, of the devil. For where you have envy and selfish ambition, there you find disorder and every evil practice. But the wisdom that comes from heaven is first of all pure; then peace-loving, considerate, submissive, full of mercy and good fruit, impartial and sincere. Peacemakers who sow in peace raise a harvest of righteousness." (James 3:13-18)

You will notice that your mind is not clear when you are holding so many things that you need to let go of. You will gain spiritual freedom and a clear mind when you take care of all that has a hold of you. Then, you will be released from emotional and spiritual pain. Follow the practice below for healing.

Reflect: When you hear destructive, critical, or judgmental voices in your mind, evaluate them to find out where they are coming from. If it is not the conviction of the Holy Spirit helping you change your attitudes and behaviors, it may be accusing spirits. The devil can accuse you and make you feel bad and depressed. Sometimes the voices you may hear are critical or judgmental toward others. If you accept the destructive, uncaring, critical voices, and believe and speak to hurt others, you will fall into sin. Sin opens the door to the devil to torment you. You will feel pain and many people don't realize that this spirit torments people. You need to repent and change your attitudes and behaviors to be freed from the spirits of torment.

Repent: When you start to lose peace and feel trapped in your foggy state of mind, find out what initiated that feeling. Many times we fight with the same demons and we need to learn to resist them with the Scripture and overcome our sinful desires. You can ask yourself. "Am I holding onto anger, blame, fear, bitterness or an unforgiving spirit?" We sometimes justify our sinful ways by holding onto them. Holding onto these will open the door for the devil to plant the seed of twisted thoughts, which will put us in a spiritual prison.

Replace: Find the Scripture to fight destructive voices. Find the Bible verse that gives you spiritual strength and direction on how to think and act to find peace with God, yourself and others.

Resist: If you suffer from spiritual oppression, rebuke the devil by saying, "You, devil, leave from me in Jesus' name. Your feeble attempt to distract me from loving God is not going to work. I choose to pray to save more people whenever you try to distract me."

Proclaim: When you struggle with destructive thoughts that try to make you lose peace, proclaim victory by saying, "I claim victory in Jesus Christ. I rejoice that God is with me and will bless me in all areas. I praise God because He loves me."

Persistent: Whenever the spirit tries to fool you with hurtful thoughts, you need to keep fighting it with the Scriptures.

Also, if the devil tries to discourage you from reading the Bible by throwing wrong thoughts and voices at you, ask the Lord to give you wisdom to read the Scriptures to learn what heavenly wisdom is about. Prayer: "Lord Jesus, help me to understand the Word of God with wisdom, knowledge, understanding and revelation from you. Help me to focus on you. Surround me with angels and protect me from all the devil's lies and distractions. Help me to love and obey you. Amen."

Spiritual Prescription

7. Listen to The Voice of God

"My sheep listen to my voice; I know them, and they follow me. I give them eternal life, and they shall never perish; no one can snatch them out of my hand." (John 10:27-28)

Our Lord Jesus likes to speak to us, and we need to make time to listen to Him. For the next 30 days, pray for 30 minutes every day. Speak to God for 15 minutes and listen to God for 15 minutes.

Prayer is communication between God and us. Many people think it is only important to talk to God, but it is more important to wait, to be still before Him, and to listen.

Invite Jesus to speak to you by saying: "Lord Jesus, please speak to me. I am listening. I love you." Clear your mind and listen in silence. Let go of your scattered thoughts and write down whatever comes to your mind. Also, write down the questions you have for God; and wait in silence. When you have an answer to a question, write it down.

It's not easy to clear your mind at first and listen, but you will be able to do it if you keep practicing. During this prayer, add your personal prayer and count the days. If you are persistent, God will let you know how He will answer your prayer.

When He says "no" to our prayer request, we need to change our prayer. When Paul's prayer was not answered the way he wanted, God gave him the reason. *"But he said to me, 'My grace is sufficient for you, for my power is made perfect in weakness.' Therefore I will boast all the more gladly about my weaknesses, so that Christ's power may rest on me."* (2 Corinthians 12:9)

Prepare your heart through a prayer of surrender: Throughout the day, pray the following prayer: "Dear Jesus, I surrender my life and everything to you. Open my heart, so I can listen to your voice. I surrender all my plans because you have better plans for me. Break my hardened heart and work in me, so I can repent of my sins. Forgive my sins and cleanse me, so that when you speak to me there will be no distractions. Jesus, I love you."

Many people who suffer from depression hear destructive voices, but they do not realize where they are coming from. Moreover, many do not learn to recognize God's voice. They need to learn how to discern voices in order for them to recognize which is from the devil and which is from the Lord. When they start recognizing God's voice in their heart and mind, they can see things more clearly and are able to see the big picture.

Recognize the origin of the voices:
There are four voices people hear in their minds, they are as follows:
(1) Other people's voices
(2) Our voice
(3) The Devil's voice
(4) The Holy Spirit's voice

Other people's voices may be something that we remember from the past, or something we heard and remember in our minds.

Our voice is our thoughts. We have freedom to make choices on which voices we will accept or resist. We have a sinful nature and sinful thoughts that can make us decide to do evil things. We also have a conscience, a new born spirit, and God-given characteristics to do good and resist sin.

The devil's voice is deceptive and destructive in nature. If we accept and follow it, we will fall into sin and can hurt ourselves and others. Many people don't know that the devil can speak to our mind, so they accept any thoughts that come to mind. That's when they are vulnerable to confused voices.

The Holy Spirit speaks to our hearts. His purpose is to teach about the Lord Jesus and prepare us to love and serve the Lord. He will try to guide and direct people to grow in faith and to help others. The Holy Spirit can use the Scriptures to lead our spiritual path and grow and also guides and directs us so we can obey the Lord. We have the freedom to obey or disobey.

Whenever thoughts come to your mind, try to acknowledge which voice you are hearing. Not all the voices are your thoughts. You need to question and ask the Lord for wisdom to discern the voices. You need to resist them, otherwise you will be confused. You need to plant the seed of God's Word in your heart so that the Holy Spirit can speak to you when you need to hear it. To recognize twisted thinking, you need to continuously read God's Word.

Many people who are depressed are bombarded with destructive voices and are having a difficult time recognizing the voice of God. When I counsel people who are depressed, I ask them to practice listening to God in silence.

It's not easy at first, but the more you practice, the easier it will be to discern voices and experience healing from confusion and overwhelming thoughts. Anything that is destructive needs to be questioned and evaluated with the Word of God so that you will not be deceived.

Spiritual Prescription

8. Develop a Relationship with the Holy Spirit

Did you know that the Holy Spirit can help healing us from depression? He certainly can. He can help us in our spiritual journey through conviction, cleansing, transformation, and healing our hearts and minds. Jesus said, *"And I will ask the Father, and he will give you another Counselor to be with you forever--'the Spirit of truth. The world cannot accept him, because it neither sees him nor knows him. But you know him, for he lives with you and will be in you. I will not leave you as orphans; I will come to you.'"* (John 14:16-18)

(1) The Holy Spirit comes to live with us when we repent and accept Jesus as our Lord and Savior. *"Peter replied, 'Repent and be baptized, every one of you, in the name of Jesus Christ for the forgiveness of your sins. And you will receive the gift of the Holy Spirit.'"* (Acts 2:38)

(2) The Holy Spirit teaches us about our Lord Jesus. *"But the Counselor, the Holy Spirit, whom the Father will send in my name, will teach you all things and will remind you of everything I have said to you."* (John 14:26) *"When the Counselor comes, whom I will send to you from the Father, the Spirit of truth who goes out from the Father, he will testify about me."* (John 15:26) *"He will bring glory to me by taking from what is mine and making it known to you."* (John 16:14)

(3) The Holy Spirit will help us to cleanse our hearts so we can grow in the Lord. *"But I tell you the truth: It is for your good that I am going away. Unless I go away, the Counselor will not come to you; but if I go, I will send him to you. When he comes, he will convict the world of guilt in regard to sin and righteousness and judgment:"* (John 16:7-8)

We need to transform our minds and hearts according to the Word of God. As we start to cleanse our spiritual house by repenting, He will start to fill our hearts with peace and joy. He will give us direction on how to help ourselves and help others grow in faith and experience healing from spiritual sicknesses, including confused thoughts and depression.

(4) He will teach us about God's values so we can see the big picture that we weren't able to see before. Hopeless feelings come when we see the world with our earthly mind, which can be affected by the devil and our sinful nature. Having the knowledge of the Word of God is critical in transforming our minds and hearts so we can learn to live a life that will please God.

(5) The Holy Spirit gives us gifts to serve others. In fact, serving others brings healing to those who are depressed and lack meaning and purpose in their life. Lack of direction in life can cause depression and despair.

(6) The Holy Spirit helps us to understand God's heart. Paul wrote, *"No eye has seen, no ear has heard, no mind has conceived what God has prepared for those who love Him – but God has revealed it to us by His Spirit." (1 Corinthians 2:9-10)* Many people who were depressed but learned to listen to the Holy Spirit have been transformed. They shared with me how the Lord blessed them with purpose and meaning. Their spirit came alive when they experienced the Holy Spirit and learned that God is alive and will speak to them.

If you have an empty feeling, you need to ask the Holy Spirit to come and fill your heart with Christ's peace and joy. Jesus asked his disciples to wait for the Holy Spirit. We should do the same.

Practice Silence

Those who have not experienced the Holy Spirit,

should try to have one hour of silence and prayer time. Ask the Holy Spirit to speak to you for a week. If you don't hear anything from the Lord, try another week and so on until you experience the Holy Spirit.

Recognize His presence by asking the Holy Spirit to give you guidance whenever you need to make a decision. In this way, you will be able to develop a relationship with the Holy Spirit who can teach, guide, comfort and direct your path. He is our spiritual counselor and until we learn to listen to the Holy Spirit and depend on His wisdom, we may be relying on our wisdom which can be affected by destructive thoughts.

Prayer: "Come Holy Spirit, come and fill my heart with your presence, peace and joy. Help me experience healing in the areas I need healing. Help me to love my Lord Jesus and help me to obey you. Cleanse my heart and my life from ungodly thoughts and behaviors. Help me to live a pure, holy life to please my Lord Jesus. Help me to understand my calling in life. Help me to obey and serve you. Amen."

Spiritual Prescription

9. Serve Others

Many people who are depressed do not have a clear goal of serving the Lord. We need to let go of our own plans and painful memories by giving them to the Lord. Paul wrote, *"I have been crucified with Christ and I no longer live, but Christ lives in me. The life I live in the body, I live by faith in the Son of God, who loved me and gave himself for me." (Galatians 2:20)* Paul didn't have the time to be depressed because his focus was serving the Lord, and not his past mistakes.

Did you know that God has plans for you? He has plans for you to use your gifts to serve others and not just yourself. As we serve others, we find meaning and purpose in life.

"'For I know the plans I have for you,' declares the Lord, 'Plans to prosper you and not to harm you, plans to give you hope and a future. Then you will call upon me and come and pray to me, and I will listen to you. You will seek me and find me when you seek me with all your heart. I will be found by you,' declares the Lord, 'and will bring you back from captivity.'" (Jeremiah 29:11-14)

God gave you the gift of life so you can use it to help others. Volunteer to help others in your community, church, or in mission. Don't ignore what God is trying to tell you. You need to understand what His plan is in order for you to be productive in God's kingdom. So, ask the Lord what you need to do to serve Him because He knows what you need to do to be fruitful.

"Then Jesus came to them and said, 'All authority in heaven and on earth has been given to me. Therefore go and make

disciples of all nations, baptizing them in the name of the Father and of the Son and of the Holy Spirit, and teaching them to obey everything I have commanded you. And surely I am with you always, to the very end of the age.'" (Matthew 28:18-20)

Paul says, *"Therefore, I urge you, brothers, in view of God's mercy, to offer your bodies as living sacrifices, holy and pleasing to God--this is your spiritual act of worship. Do not conform any longer to the pattern of this world, but be transformed by the renewing of your mind. Then you will be able to test and approve what God's will is--his good, pleasing and perfect will. For by the grace given me I say to every one of you: Do not think of yourself more highly than you ought, but rather think of yourself with sober judgment, in accordance with the measure of faith God has given you. Just as each of us has one body with many members, and these members do not all have the same function, so in Christ we who are many form one body, and each member belongs to all the others. We have different gifts, according to the grace given us. If a man's gift is prophesying, let him use it in proportion to his faith. If it is serving, let him serve; if it is teaching, let him teach; if it is encouraging, let him encourage; if it is contributing to the needs of others, let him give generously; if it is leadership, let him govern diligently; if it is showing mercy, let him do it cheerfully."* (Romans 12:1-8)

Listen to the Holy Spirit to find out how you can be generous with your gifts whether it is words of encouragement or sharing your wealth to help the poor. Our blessings come from sharing what we have received.

God can use your painful experiences. He can bring healing in your heart. You can tell others how God has healed you from depression. He delivered me from depression, grief and pain. I never went back to my depression pit because He taught me the lesson of finding the way out through the Word of the Lord. I found joy in loving and serving the Lord. I have seen many miracles in my ministry and that teaches me that God can do so much more than what I think or imagine and I don't have to live in pain.

Prayer: "Lord Jesus, I want to know your plans, visions, and dreams for me. Please help me to know how I can make disciples of Jesus. Help me to understand my gifts so I can serve you to the fullest. Help me to look up to you and serve you so I don't hide my gifts but use them to the maximum for your kingdom and to help the poor. Please open doors for me and help me to connect with people who can help me use my gifts to serve you. Help me find joy in serving you. Give me wisdom so I will be able to obey you."

Spiritual Prescription

10. Proclaim Victory in Christ

We need to envision our future with hope in any circumstances because God is going to help us. Sometimes traumatic events in our lives take away the peace and joy we are promised in Christ. Hurts and pain can hinder us from seeing the victorious picture that God wants us to see. God is so close to us even when we are hurting badly and He has created us to have victories lives. *"In this world you will have trouble. But take heart! I have overcome the world." (John 16:33b) "But thanks be to God! He gives us the victory through our Lord Jesus Christ." (1 Corinthians 15:57) "for everyone born of God overcomes the world. This is the victory that has overcome the world, even our faith. Who is it that overcomes the world? Only he who believes that Jesus is the Son of God." (1 John 5:4-5)*

God's Word has so much power and can save and heal those who trust in Him. We need to develop a habit of proclaiming God's victory every day even in our painful times. We need to develop a habit of thinking and saying things that we want to see based on the Word of God. We need to have faith that could move mountains. Keep praying that you will have that faith.

Knowing the Scriptures is the beginning of your journey of victories in life. Also, you need to know that your words have so much power that God can help you see the mountain move. Therefore, get rid of defeating words and start proclaiming God's love, blessings, and faith, especially in times of worry, fear, despair, disappointment, discouragement and devastation. Praise and thank God for His deliverance and healing when you feel like there is no hope. Anticipate God holding hands with you if you feel like you are failing because He cares for you, your family, and your everyday affairs.

Claiming victory has been one of my practices whenever I am worried, disappointed, discouraged or wonder why God doesn't seem to answer my prayers quickly. It gives me the right perspective and helps me to handle difficulties with God's wisdom which comes from the Word of God. We should start proclaiming victory in Christ so our helpless situations become learning situations. God can use us to teach others about His power and compassion.

I learned to proclaim victory because it helped me to handle my anxiety attacks. After a car accident on an icy road, I occasionally experienced panic attacks when I was on icy roads and even when I was not on the icy road. At those times, I started repeating the Lord's prayer over and over until I found peace. At the same time, I try to avoid icy roads and try not to put myself in situations where I might suffer an anxiety attack. Eventually, I wrote a prayer of victory to be healed from anxiety attacks. Whenever the spirits of fear and anxiety try to take over my mind, I claim victory in Christ. This prayer has helped me immensely and I have not had an anxiety attack since I started proclaiming victory in Christ. Write your own prayer of victory and start proclaiming it. Here is the victory prayer I wrote:

1. A victory prayer for myself

I claim victory that I made a decision to love Jesus.
He is the first priority in my life.
I claim victory for God because He has the ultimate power over everything in my life, no one else does.
I claim victory for making a commitment to serve Christ.

I claim victory over my guilt and shame so that all my sins are washed away by the blood of Jesus Christ
I claim victory that God is the source of my love, peace, wisdom, joy, and strength.
I claim victory over my future belief that
God is going to bless me beyond my imagination.
I claim victory because I decided to love Jesus more than my sinful desires and passion.
I claim victory over all my problems and concerns
so that I am continuously surrendering everything to God.
I claim victory that I made a decision to bless and forgive those who have hurt me.
I claim victory over my fears because God is guiding
my spiritual path.
I claim victory over my life challenges knowing that
God is going to give me wisdom to handle it.

2. A victory prayer for my family

I claim victory that God will take care of my family
for His glory.
I claim victory that my family will be filled with
the Holy Spirit and serve God to the fullest.
I claim victory that God will give my children spiritual blessings beyond my imagination.
I claim victory for my children that God will provide what they need, including godly mentors.
I claim victory that my family will be blessed with
spiritual gifts and use them for God's glory.
I claim victory that God will take care of my family
when I cannot take care of them.
I claim victory that God will protect my family and
help them grow in faith.
I claim victory that other people will be blessed by
my family's presence and ministry.

3. A victory prayer for my ministry

I claim victory that God will provide an opportunity for me to spread the gospel of Jesus much more than I have ever imagined.
I claim victory that with God's help, I will be able to help others use their spiritual gifts to the maximum for God's glory.
I claim victory that the Holy Spirit will bring powerful Christian leaders to join me in building up the kingdom of God to win many lost souls and grow spiritually.
I claim victory that God will help me use my time wisely to reach out to those who are in spiritual bondage, so they can find spiritual freedom in Christ.
I claim victory because I am continuously surrendering all my plans and desires in order to love and serve Christ.
I claim victory in managing financial resources with God's wisdom so that I will glorify God with my resources and help others to be saved and find hope and healing in Christ.
I claim victory that the Holy Spirit will anoint me so much that others will experience the Holy Spirit's healing presence through my ministry and book projects.
I claim victory that when God has different ministry plans for my life, I will obey Him because His plans are always better than mine.
I claim victory over my selfishness that I will look after Jesus' interest, knowing that is the only way to build up Christ's kingdom.
I claim victory because I will be focusing all my gifts, time, energy on loving Jesus and serving Him to the fullest.

Chapter 8

What Helps for Recovery

- Praying
- Reading and meditating of the Bible
- Giving all problems to the Lord
- Having faith in God's grace and forgiveness
- Forgiving myself and others
- Having contact with positive, trustworthy people
- Laughing, humor
- Having someone to talk to, knowing that people care
- Understanding the signs in my dreams and in life
- Praise and worship services
- Singing the gospel or hearing the Lord's Word
- Reading inspirational books
- Having faith in God
- Finding hope in the Word of God
- Writing poetry
- Not dwelling in the past
- Knowing that life is a gift from God
- Thinking positive
- Doing something that makes me think differently
- Having family support
- Seeing that Jesus is my medication for depression
- Having faith that depression has been removed
- Professional counseling
- Taking anti-depression medicine
- Inspirational music
- My children's presence
- Claiming victory in Christ
- Writing a journal
- Finding a job that they like
- Removing yourself from abusive situations

Chapter 9

An Invitation

1. An Invitation to Accept Christ

Do you have an empty heart that cannot be filled with anyone or anything? God can fill your empty heart with His love and forgiveness. Do you feel your life has no meaning, no direction, no purpose, and you don't know where to turn to find the answers? It's time to turn to God because that's the only way you can understand the meaning and purpose of your life. You will find a direction that will lead you to fulfillment and joy. Is your heart broken and hurting? Do you know how to experience healing? Until we meet Christ in our hearts, we cannot find the peace and healing that God can provide. Jesus can help heal your broken heart. If you don't have a relationship with Christ, this is an opportunity for you to accept Jesus into your heart so you can be saved and find peace and healing from God. Here is a prayer if you are ready to accept Jesus:

"Dear Jesus, I surrender my life and everything to you. I give you my pain, fear, regret, resentment, anger, worry, and concerns that overwhelm me. I am a sinner. I need your forgiveness. Please come into my heart and my life and forgive my sins. I believe that you died for my sins and that you have plans for my life. Please heal my broken heart and bless me with your peace and joy. Help me cleanse my life so I can live a godly life. Help me understand your plans for my life and help me obey you. Fill me with the Holy Spirit, and guide me so I can follow your way. I pray this in Jesus' name. Amen."

2. An Invitation for The Transformation Project Prison Ministry (TPPM).

Chaplain Yong Hui V. McDonald has been in prison ministry since 1999. She started working as a chaplain at Adams County Detention Facility (ACDF) in Brighton, Colorado, in 2003. She started the Transformation Project Prison Ministry (TPPM) in 2005 in an effort to bring spiritually nurturing books to the inmates at the facility because the chaplains' office had a shortage of inspirational books. In the process, Maximum Saints books and DVDs were produced by ACDF inmates for the other inmates.

The Maximum Saints books and DVDs project provides the ACDF incarcerated saints an opportunity, and offers encouragement, to put their writing and artistic skills to use to provide hope, peace, restoration, and healing. It also gives spiritual support to incarcerated people, the homeless, as well as to interested persons outside the prisons. Maximum Saints are not necessarily classified as maximum security inmates; they are called Maximum Saints because they are using their gifts to the maximum to help others.

"One Million Dream Project"

Books and DVDs produced by TPPM are distributed in many jails, prisons, and homeless shelters nationwide free of charge and are made possible by grants and donations. America has 2.3 million people incarcerated, the largest prison population in the world, and there is a great shortage of inspirational books in many jails and prisons.

In 2010, TPPM board decided to expand their ministry goal and started, "One Million Dream Project." TPPM decided to raise enough funds to distribute one million copies of each book TPPM produces for prisoners and homeless people. I ask you to pray for this project so God can help TPPM reach out to those who cannot speak for themselves but are in need of spiritual guidance from the Lord. TPPM is a 501(c)(3) nonprofit organization so your donation is 100% tax deductible. If you would like to be a partner in this very important mission of bringing transformation through the message of Christ in prisons and homeless shelters or want to know more about this project, go to our website. You can donate online or you can write a check addressed to: Transformation Project Prison Ministry and send it to the following address:

Transformation Project Prison Ministry
5209 Montview Boulevard
Denver, CO 80207

Website: www.transformprisons.org
720-951-2629
You can find us on Facebook.